Thomas Jefferson

ARCHITECT OF DEMOCRACY

Thomas Jefferson

ARCHITECT OF DEMOCRACY

BY JOHN B. SEVERANCE

CLARION BOOKS / NEW YORK

PICTURE CREDITS

All illustrations not specifically credited below were furnished by
The Library of Congress, Washington, D. C.

Culver Pictures. Inc.: pages 26, 33, 43, 48, 86, 87, 92, 104, 107 (top and bottom),
113, 114, 117 (left and right), 135, 140, 145 (bottom), 146, 149, 153, 170.
Sylvia Frezzolini Severance: pages 81 and 143.

FRONTISPIECE:

An engraving based on the portrait of Thomas Jefferson
painted by Charles Willson Peale in 1791.

CLARION BOOKS
a Houghton Mifflin Company imprint
215 Park Avenue South, New York, NY 10003
Text copyright © 1998 by John B. Severance

Text is 13-point Bembo
Book design by Sylvia Frezzolini Severance

Printed in the USA

LIBRARY OF CONGRESS CATALOGING-IN-PUBLICATION DATA
Severance, John B.
Thomas Jefferson : architect of democracy / by John B. Severance.
p.   cm.
Summary: Explores the life of the third president, from his childhood in Virginia, through
his involvement in the Revolutionary War, to his years in office.
ISBN 0-395-84513-0
1. Jefferson, Thomas, 1743–1826—Juvenile literature. 2. Presidents—United States—Biography—
Juvenile literature. 3. United States—Politics and government—1775–1783—Juvenile literature.
4. United States—Politics and government—1783–1809—Juvenile literature.
[1. Jefferson, Thomas, 1743–1826. 2. Presidents.] I. Title.
E332.79.S48   1998
973.4'8'092—dc21   97-31010
[B]   CIP
                                                           AC

KPT 10 9 8 7 6 5 4 3 2 1

To the memory of my parents:
Frank, a lawyer,
and Frances, an artist.
Both admired the versatile
intellect of Thomas Jefferson.

Contents

The Committee for Drafting the Declaration of Independence.
Jefferson, seated in the middle, holds up a paper.

CHAPTER ONE

Jefferson in His Era

If he wanted to run for office today, Thomas Jefferson, third president of the United States, might not get elected. The author of the Declaration of Independence probably had no trouble writing the speech for his first inauguration on March 4, 1801. Reading it in the Senate Chamber of the unfinished Capitol was another matter. His subdued voice was hardly heard beyond the third row of the audience. Microphones had not been invented and electricity was not yet a source of power. Perhaps it was a good thing for President Jefferson that, in his lifetime, newspapers were the main means of public communication. It had been a close election. If radio and television had been invented, he might not have impressed the nation at all. Although he was a clever player in the game of politics, this quiet philosopher preferred the privacy of life at Monticello, the elegant home he designed and built on a mountain in the Piedmont region of Virginia.

Monticello, Jefferson's home near the Blue Ridge Mountains.

Another fact about Jefferson would have upset modern voters. He owned slaves. Slavery was common throughout the colonies. Except for Quakers, few voters in the new nation cared strongly if a candidate happened to be a slave owner. Blacks could not vote and neither could women. In fact, in the original colonies, the only people who could vote were men who owned property. Most men of Jefferson's time thought of slaves and even women as a kind of property.

Actually, Thomas Jefferson was opposed to the idea of slavery. Before the Revolution, he proposed a plan for the emancipation of slaves to the House of Burgesses, the colonial legislature of Virginia, but both the royal governor and the king's council in England rejected the proposal. In the first draft of the Declaration of Independence presented to Congress, Jefferson deplored slavery as a "cruel war against human nature itself, violating its most sacred rights of life and liberty." Southern slave owners and New England slave traders in the Continental Congress insisted that this passage be eliminated. In 1781, Jefferson included a bill for emancipation in a package of suggested legislative reform for the Commonwealth of Virginia. That particular bill got lost in committee studies. After the Revolution he tried to get a bill through the U.S. Congress to gradually abolish slavery but it failed. In his autobiography begun in 1821, he wrote of slaves, "Nothing is more certainly written in the book of fate, than that these people are to be free."

Slaves working in a field. The job of the man with the gun at his knees is to scare away birds that might eat the seeds being planted.

Jefferson depended on his own slaves to build and maintain Monticello. On his deathbed he freed five of his house slaves who could earn their livings by trades they had learned, but he believed it was cruel to free illiterate slaves who would not be able to support themselves. "To give liberty, or rather to abandon persons whose habits have been formed in slavery," he wrote to a friend, "is like abandoning children." A modern biographer of Jefferson, Fawn Brodie, says we must not judge him harshly for attitudes toward women and blacks that were different from those we hold today. "One should not blame Jefferson for falling short of perfection as a liberator of the human spirit," she wrote. "He continued . . . to follow traditions . . . that were in his time practically universal. After his death, his . . . intellectual legacy served to aid the liberation of both women and blacks."

That legacy includes a number of significant documents and events. For example, Jefferson helped his friend the marquis de Lafayette, a French soldier and statesman who had fought alongside George Washington in the American Revolution, write a document called a Declaration of Rights in support of the French Revolution. In the nineteenth century, revolutions in the Spanish colonies of Latin America were inspired by Jefferson's words. More than a century and a half after the writing of the Declaration of Independence, its language influenced the wording of a declaration written for India in 1930 by Mahatma Gandhi.

As president, Jefferson authorized the Louisiana Purchase in 1803, expanding United States territory from the Mississippi River to the Rocky Mountains. His main purpose in doubling the area of the country was to keep Napoleon Bonaparte, then ruler of France, from establishing a claim on the American continent through New Orleans.

Left: Simón Bolívar, who, from 1819 to 1824, liberated Spanish colonies that are now Venezuela, Colombia, Ecuador, Bolivia, and Peru. Right: The marquis de Lafayette, Jefferson's friend, was active in the French Revolution.

This move avoided a costly war with France that might have forced the United States to seek help from its recent enemy, Great Britain. The life of the young country might have been snuffed out just when it was taking its place among the nations of the world.

Jefferson anticipated another threat from Great Britain. In 1793, a Scottish fur trader named Alexander Mackenzie had crossed the Canadian wilderness to reach the Pacific Ocean. As a result of his exploration, Mackenzie recommended to the British government that a chain of forts and fur-trading posts be established across the continent. When President Jefferson learned of this in 1802, he sprang into action to begin preparations for the Lewis and Clark expedition. His

Lewis and Clark meet with western Indians.

intention was to establish an American presence in the west to keep the British Empire out. New English colonies on the Pacific coast might have created a serious political threat to the recently established United States.

Yet Jefferson disliked politics. He served two terms as president of the United States not because he loved power but because he wanted to help the new nation survive its infancy. In fact, the office of president was not then regarded as a position of great power because the United States was not a powerful nation. To Jefferson, his presidency was not the most significant part of his life. His best-known biographer, Dumas Malone, wrote, "Not only was he an intensely devoted family man; he was a friend to mankind. Although rooted in his native soil he never ceased to contemplate the universe." The words Jefferson wished to have carved on his tombstone "and not a word more" were, "Here was buried Thomas Jefferson, Author of the Declaration of American Independence, of the Statute of Virginia for religious freedom, and the Father of the University of Virginia."

Jefferson's instructions for his gravestone.

Thomas Jefferson as a young man.

CHAPTER TWO
An Enlightening Education

Virginia, named in honor of Queen Elizabeth I of England, the Virgin Queen, was the first and the largest of the English colonies in North America. Since Europeans had no idea of the size of the continent between the Atlantic and Pacific Oceans, early boundary descriptions were vague. A royal commercial charter granted to the Virginia Company in 1609 claimed land "from sea to sea." Before the American Revolution the area called Virginia came to mean the land that now includes the states of Virginia, West Virginia, and Kentucky. During the Revolution, a military expedition sponsored by Governor Patrick Henry added the area now including Ohio, Indiana, Illinois, and Michigan to Virginia's territory.

Although Virginia was vast, the earliest agriculture and commerce took place in settlements on the eastern seaboard. The first tobacco plantations were established along the rivers in the low country near the Atlantic Ocean known as the Tidewater region. Westward, in the

A tobacco plantation.

forested hill country between the Tidewater and the Blue Ridge Mountains, is an area called the Piedmont. About 1737, on the western edge of the Piedmont wilderness, within sight of the mountains, Peter Jefferson, a tall, powerful frontiersman and surveyor, built a one-and-a-half-story farmhouse overlooking the Rivanna River. He called it Shadwell after the district in London where his wife, Jane Randolph, had been born. Indians, who sometimes appeared out of the deep forest to visit, were their only neighbors.

In April 1743, Peter and Jane's third child and first son, Thomas, was born. According to the calendar then in use in England and the colonies, the date was April 2, 1743, o.s., or Old Style. Nine years later, the more accurate New Style calendar, used in continental Europe, was adopted, and today Jefferson's birthday is celebrated on April 13. Tom's earliest memory was of being lifted up to sit on a pillow in front of a slave riding a horse. The family was moving to a plantation on the James River called Tuckahoe. Before the owner, Jane's cousin William Randolph, died, he had asked his best friend, Peter Jefferson, to manage the estate for his orphaned children and see to their education. The Randolph children, two Jefferson sisters, young Tom, and several cousins were taught reading, writing, and arithmetic in a little one-room schoolhouse on the Tuckahoe grounds. The slave children were not allowed to go to school.

Tom's father taught him riding, fishing, hunting, swimming, and surveying. For the rest of his life, although he was not such a robust woodsman as his father, he continued to enjoy hiking and riding horseback. His older sister Jane taught him to appreciate the animals and plants of the fields and forests when they rambled together in the countryside. This was probably the beginning of his interest in natural history and science. Jane also taught Tom music and was the first to encourage his lifelong love of books. Music led him to become an excellent violinist and his love of books made him one of the best-educated men in the thirteen colonies.

Tom's fascination with architecture may have begun in 1752, when the family moved back to Shadwell. By then there were six Jefferson children and the simple farmhouse had to be expanded. A new mill was built as well as other outbuildings. Shadwell must have been in a constant state of change. The resonant clattering of lumber, the rhythmical rasping of handsaws, and the steady banging of hammers would have been another sort of music to Tom's ears. He watched attentively. For the rest of his life he loved the clamor of building as well as the mathematics and design that went with it.

The noise and dust of construction were interrupted for Tom when he was sent off to the school of the Reverend William Douglas to learn Greek, Latin, and French. When he was an old man, Jefferson wrote in his autobiography that his teacher was actually not very good at Latin or Greek "but with the rudiments of these languages he taught me the French." Even that achievement was somewhat limited. Because the Reverend Mr. Douglas came from Scotland, Tom's French was tinged with a Scottish accent. This was not much of an embarrassment until many years later when Jefferson lived in Paris as the United States ambassador to France.

In the summer of 1757, Peter Jefferson died. Tom was shocked. In his grief he buried himself in his music and his books. But his father left him well-off. According to an English tradition called primogeniture, a Virginia gentleman normally willed all his wealth and property to his eldest son. This left other family members, including the widow, living on the edge of poverty. Peter Jefferson ignored this custom and gave each of his children a portion of his lands and money. To his widow he left the use of Shadwell for the rest of her life. As the eldest son, however, Tom still received the lion's share of his father's estate, which made him fairly wealthy at the age of fourteen.

Peter Jefferson's dying wish had been for his son to continue his education. In 1758 the guardians named in Peter's will and Tom's mother arranged for him to be sent to a small school run by the Reverend James Maury. The school was on Mr. Maury's plantation, fourteen miles from Shadwell. There were eight students in addition to Mr. Maury's own eight children. On weekends Tom rode back to Shadwell to help his mother with the business and the social life of the plantation. He resented the responsibility and this may have led to a coolness he seems to have felt toward his mother at this time. To relieve his boredom with life at Shadwell, Tom often brought a schoolmate along. Frequently his hunting and hiking companion was Mr. Maury's son James, and sometimes it was his good friend Dabney Carr.

The Reverend Mr. Maury's large household and library made a home that Tom preferred to Shadwell. Here he learned various methods of study. For example, to observe natural history, Mr. Maury took his students on field trips into the mountains. But the use of language was the most important subject taught by Mr. Maury. He once wrote to his son urging him to "digest what you read, to enter into the spirit and design of your author, to observe every step he takes . . . and to dwell on any remarkable beauties of diction . . . or masterly strokes of true wit." Tom must have learned the same concepts in his study of classical authors, which he read in the original Greek and Latin. This led the future author of the Declaration of Independence to develop a fine writing style of his own.

The tall and slender reddish-haired boy may have seemed much too serious to some people, but that made it all the more amusing when he set up sly pranks. One time, his friends at school were astonished to learn that Tom had accepted a challenge to race his fat old mare against Dabney Carr's fast young horse. There was a lot of laughing and joking about Tom's foolishness until someone noticed that Jefferson had written on the agreement that the ridiculous race was to take place on February 30.

When he was sixteen Jefferson wrote to his guardian, John Harvie, that he wished to further his education. This was partly an effort to get away from Shadwell but he was also seriously interested in adding to his knowledge and learning more about the world. "By going to the College," he wrote, "I shall get a more universal acquaintance. . . . I can pursue my studies in the Greek and Latin . . . and likewise learn something of the Mathematics." To anyone living in Virginia, "the College" meant William and Mary in Williamsburg, the capital of the colony. In March 1760, Tom Jefferson left the Piedmont region for the first time in his life. He rode his horse at a leisurely pace beside a wagon driven by his slave Jupiter, following the one hundred and fifty miles of dirt road that led through the woods to Williamsburg. Along the way he stopped for two weeks at a Tidewater plantation to enjoy a round of parties and dances. It was here he first met Patrick Henry, a married

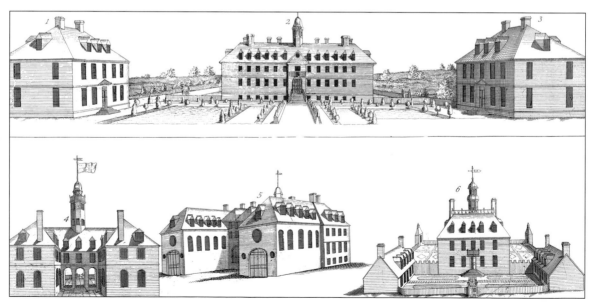

Illustrations of Williamsburg found in England at the Bodleian Library, Oxford.

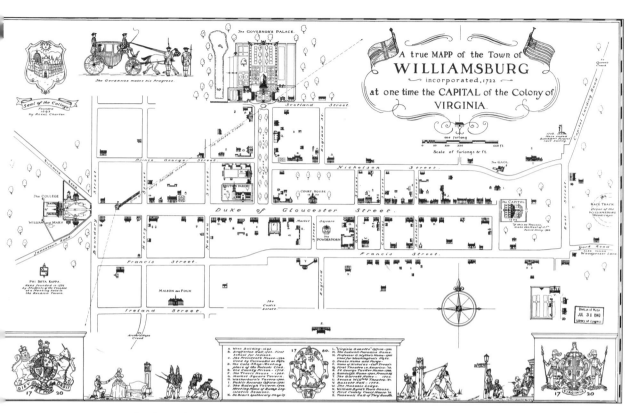

A map of colonial Williamsburg.

man who had already failed as both farmer and storekeeper but who would later become a significant name in the politics of the American Revolution. The older man was more outgoing and rough cut than Jefferson but the two became good friends for a time.

The traffic in colonial Williamsburg was made up of horseback riders, farm wagons, and elegant carriages all crowded onto one wide, unpaved, mile-long main road called Duke of Gloucester Street. At the western end were the three buildings of the College of William and Mary. There were only seven teachers on the faculty, but most had come there from prestigious English universities. One of them made a deep impression on the new student. "Dr. William Small of Scotland," wrote Jefferson in his autobiography, "was then professor of mathematics, a man profound in most of the useful branches of science . . . and from his conversation I got my first views of . . . the system of things in which we are placed."

It was probably Dr. Small who helped Tom study the important thinkers of the intellectual revolution called the Enlightenment, which had been going on in Europe during the seventeenth and eighteenth centuries. Three of the earlier Enlightenment philosophers, Francis Bacon, Isaac Newton, and John Locke, became Jefferson's intellectual heroes. He must also have heard of a number of the later ones, especially Jean Jacques Rousseau, regarded by many historians as the intellectual father of the French Revolution. The basic thinking of the Enlightenment, sometimes called the Age of Reason, was that people are born naturally good. It is therefore possible for them to learn how to borrow from the laws of nature to establish government for the good of everyone. The enemies of this kind of reasoning were intolerance, censorship, and dictatorial authority.

For the author of the Declaration of Independence, the greatest Enlightenment influence came from the ideas of John Locke. In his *Essay Concerning Human Understanding,* Locke explained his belief that each of us begins life with a blank mind waiting to be educated. In a state of nature, all beings are happy, reasonable, equal, and independent. No one has the right to hurt anyone else. The happiness of each individual, Locke thought, could be extended by cooperation to insure the happiness and well-being of a whole community. The key was enlightened and rational education. If everyone studied the laws of nature, soci-

Top: Enlightenment philosophers Sir Francis Bacon (left) and Sir Isaac Newton (right). Bottom: Jean Jacques Rousseau, intellectual father of the French Revolution.

ety would be fit to govern itself by the consent of the people in it. But some individuals learn to scorn the laws of nature and become hurtful to others. Locke thought that when hurtful people try to impose a system of tyranny on society, the people should band together to revolt against the tyranny. From his readings in Mr. Maury's school Thomas Jefferson became skilled in using the English language. From his studies at the College of William and Mary he began to develop the ideas he would later put into the language of the Declaration of Independence.

The sounds of language were also important to Jefferson although he was not much of a speaker himself. One moonlit night in the spring of 1762 he heard a Cherokee Indian chief from Tennessee make a farewell speech to his tribe. Chief Outasseté, who was passing through Williamsburg on his way to visit King George III of England, had been the guest of honor at a dinner held at the college. Afterward,

Cherokee chief Outasseté was admired by Jefferson.

John Locke,
one of Jefferson's
intellectual heroes.

Tom was deeply impressed by the sound and style of the chief's voice
and the respectful silence it inspired in his fellow tribesmen as they listened while seated around their campfires. The vivid memory lasted
into old age when Jefferson wrote to John Adams that although
Outasseté had filled him with awe, "I did not understand a word he
uttered."

In that same year Tom began his study of law. He was probably
inspired by John Locke's essay called *Some Thoughts Concerning Education*. "It would be strange to suppose an English gentleman should
be ignorant of the laws of his country," wrote Locke. He believed that
a knowledge of law was essential for people participating in their own
government. Dr. Small also influenced the new direction of study. At
the palace of the colonial governor, where Tom sometimes played the

George Wythe, Jefferson's mentor and friend.

fiddle at parties, Small introduced him to the most brilliant lawyer in Virginia, George Wythe. The remarkable mind of the tall and lanky student made such an impression on the lawyer that before long Jefferson, Small, Wythe, and Governor Francis Fauquier, also a well-educated man, were often a foursome at elegant dinners hosted by the governor. In his autobiography, Jefferson wrote, "To the habitual conversations on these occasions I owed much instruction. Mr. Wythe continued to be my . . . mentor in youth, and my most affectionate friend through life. In 1767, he led me into the practice of law . . . at which I continued until the Revolution shut up the courts of justice."

Although he spent more hours at his studies than most students at the college, Tom found plenty of time to attend concerts and dances at the Governor's Palace. It was probably at one of these events in 1762 that he first saw sixteen-year-old Rebecca Burwell, the sister of one of his classmates. The awkward young student was so bashful that he was unable to speak to her for nearly a year. Instead he wrote about her to another classmate, John Page. He finally got up enough courage to ask her for her portrait in profile cut out of paper. He placed this inside the back of his pocket watch just as people now put photos of their loved ones in their wallets. He was heartbroken when his bedroom ceiling leaked rainwater on the watch one night and ruined the paper image of Rebecca. He was afraid to ask her for a replacement and instead wrote more frustrated letters to his friend Page.

In October 1763, Tom danced with Rebecca Burwell at a party at the Raleigh Tavern in Williamsburg. When he tried to talk with her, his tangled sentences were punctuated with gaps of silence. Sometime in the winter of 1764, he had a more coherent conversation with Rebecca in which he suggested that the two of them might become engaged. She would have to wait, however, while he went on a previously planned trip to Europe, stopping in Italy to buy a good fiddle. Tom never went on the trip but Rebecca found the idea of waiting absurd and later decided to marry someone else. The rejection brought on one of the agonizing migraine headaches that would continue to plague Jefferson during stressful times for the rest of his life.

Perhaps it was a relief to Tom that, in spite of his emotional turmoil, he was able to continue his legal studies. There were no law schools in the colonies and many students went to London to study at the Inns of Court. Another way to prepare for the bar exams was to work with a successful and established lawyer. George Wythe had done this in his student days and Tom Jefferson now chose to study under Wythe in the same way. Both Jefferson and Wythe had meticulous and thorough-going minds. As a result Jefferson was much slower in the study of law than his friend Patrick Henry.

Henry had arrived in Williamsburg shortly after Jefferson. He claimed he had done enough reading to sit for the bar exam. All the examiners except George Wythe were charmed by Henry's flamboyant talk. Although he clearly had not done enough reading to qualify, the other examiners accepted his promise to read further and admitted him to the bar. He soon became one of the most successful courtroom lawyers in Virginia. He settled in the backwoods, where he became so popular that he was elected to the House of Burgesses. As a plainly dressed backwoodsman, Henry often irritated the more refined Tidewater burgesses with his dramatic style of speaking. By April 1765 he had already established a reputation as a noisy hothead when word reached Williamsburg that the English Parliament had passed a stamp tax on the American colonies.

All public papers such as legal documents, licenses, newspapers, brochures, and even playing cards were to have special stamps attached showing that a tax had been paid. The British government was desperate for revenue after the Seven Years War of 1756–63. This monumental struggle, known in America as the French and Indian War, was primarily a disastrous contest between England and France for control of North America. It had devastated most of Europe, especially France, and had nearly bankrupted England. Since the colonies benefited from the protection of the British army and navy it seemed natural to Parliament that the colonies should pay for part of the cost. But the colonies saw the matter differently. Although England had always

A skirmish in the French and Indian War.

levied customs duties on goods shipped into colonial seaports, this was the first time Parliament had ever tried to establish a tax on local goods produced and sold within the colonies. Until now only the colonial legislatures had had the authority to levy internal taxes upon themselves. On the other side of the Atlantic, people living in the English counties were represented in Parliament and could have some say about their taxes. The American colonies, however, had no representation in England.

At first this problem did not seem to concern the House of

Patrick Henry was a dramatic orator in the House of Burgesses.

Burgesses. No one wanted to risk being accused of treason by questioning the British government. Late in May 1765, Patrick Henry decided to raise the issue. In a ringing speech that apparently aroused the stuffy Tidewater burgesses, he insisted that only the legislature of the colony had the right to tax the people of Virginia. As he reached a crescendo, some of the burgesses interrupted with shouts of "Treason! Treason!" "If this be treason," Henry concluded, "make the most of it!"

Because no one was taking notes, some historians think that Henry did not actually say this. In one way, his exact words are not important. By the end of summer, reports of the defiant speech had spread, and the legislatures of nine of the thirteen colonies had resolved that they, and only they, had the right to levy internal taxes. The ten years of resistance to British authority that would lead finally to the Battle of Lexington and the first shots of the American Revolution had been touched off by Patrick Henry's fiery words. In the crowd at the doorway of the House of Burgesses, Tom Jefferson stood listening.

The Battle of Lexington.

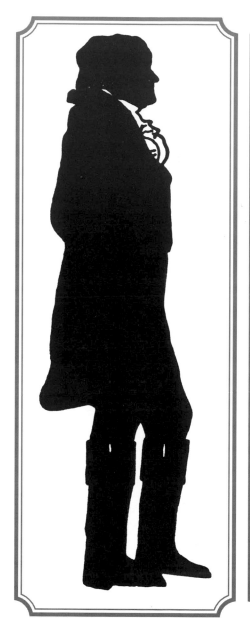

Silhouettes of Thomas and Martha Wayles Jefferson.

CHAPTER THREE

The Road to Revolution

In 1768, Thomas Jefferson was elected to the House of Burgesses. A lot had happened in his life during the few years since he had stood listening to Patrick Henry's condemnation of the Stamp Act. He had taken over the management of his inherited land. His sister Martha married his close friend Dabney Carr. His older and favorite sister, Jane, died in the fall of 1765. Jefferson planted flowers in her memory at Shadwell in the spring of 1766 and then, for the first time in his life, left the colony. The trip was partly intended to soothe his grief over Jane's death but it also had other purposes. In Annapolis, Jefferson visited the Maryland legislature. In a letter to John Page he described the noise and confusion he saw. "I was surprised to see them address the speaker . . . three, four, and five at a time," Jefferson wrote. "In short every thing seemed to be carried without the house in general's knowing what was proposed." Another purpose of the trip was to visit Philadelphia, the center of medical studies in the colonies, to have himself inoculated against smallpox. The new and controversial procedure was against the law in Virginia and many of the other colonies. Jefferson went on to visit New York and then sailed home. In the next three years he built up a successful law practice with clients throughout the colony. He also bought and sold land to improve his estates and began leveling a building site for his own house on a mountaintop near Shadwell.

Not long after Jefferson took his seat in the House of Burgesses on April 6, 1769, he made his first effort for emancipation of slaves. He did not suggest freeing the entire slave population at once. He simply proposed to make it legal for a slave owner to free a slave by recording the event at the county court. The older burgesses were incensed that the twenty-six-year-old newcomer dared to upset tradition. The new royal governor, Norborne Berkeley, baron de Botetourt, rejected the proposal and so did the King's Council in London. The issue became overshadowed by the escalating tension between the colonies and Britain over the Townshend Acts of 1767.

Named for Charles Townshend, a British cabinet minister, these acts levied taxes on all tea, lead, glass, and paints imported into the colonies. The revenues from these taxes were not used to cover expenses of governing the colonies but were sent back to England. In 1768 tensions increased throughout the colonies and the angry accusation of taxation without representation was heard once again. With the encouragement of Samuel Adams, a Bostonian who had inspired riots protesting the Stamp Act of 1765, the Massachusetts legislature circulated a letter to the other legislatures urging a united front against the Townshend Acts. Parliament retaliated by ruling that all such letters were acts of treason for which the writers could be taken to

England for trial. The House of Burgesses then reasserted their sole right to levy taxes in Virginia. They also resolved that seeking colonial unity, as Massachusetts had done, could not be considered treason and added that trials for treason, or any other crime, should take place within the colony, not in England. Finally, they ordered that these resolutions be circulated among the other colonial legislatures with a request for concurrence. Governor Botetourt promptly dissolved the Virginia legislature.

Governor Botetourt was actually a genial and reasonable man but he had to obey his standing instructions from the British government. The ex-lawmakers, however, refused to be put down by rules issued from England. They simply reconvened at the Raleigh Tavern. Under the leadership of fellow burgesses George Washington, George Mason, and Richard Henry Lee, they drew up the Virginia Resolves, which were based on resolutions made earlier in the Pennsylvania legislature. The purpose of the resolves was to put pressure on the economy of Great Britain by refusing to buy imports from England. The long list of forbidden items included food, liquor, furniture, paper, leather goods, and various kinds of cloth. At elegant parties in Williamsburg, clothing made of homespun soon replaced the customary silks and satins. Traditionally, most colonists had thought of themselves as Englishmen. They were now beginning to think of themselves as Americans.

On February 1, 1770, the Shadwell house burned to the ground. At the time, Jefferson was three miles away on business in Charlottesville. A slave came to tell him that, although no one was hurt, everything was lost except Tom's fiddle. With all of his personal notes, legal papers, and precious law books reduced to smoldering ashes, Jefferson was deeply concerned about the serious problem of how to reconstruct his law practice. He seemed to forget that his mother and his four teenage siblings would have to spend the rest of the winter living in the outbuildings of the farm. To his friend Page he wrote that if the construction of Monticello had not already begun, "I might have cherished . . . thoughts of leaving these my native hills."

Living in rented rooms in Charlottesville, Jefferson planned the hauling of construction materials to his lofty site. His friends and neighbors found it odd that he was building his mansion on the top of a mountain. Traditionally, the Tidewater plantations and Piedmont farms were settled on flat land along rivers, where the soil was rich and

An early version of Monticello, without the dome that was added later.

water transportation handy. Jefferson had to make careful calculations for all the foundation stones, framing lumber, and limestone for mortar that had to be carted in wagons up steep slopes. Even the water for molding bricks and mixing mortar had to be hauled up in huge barrels called hogsheads. The building of Monticello and the planting of its surrounding acreage became a continuing effort that would occupy Jefferson on and off for the rest of his life. The artist in him rejoiced in the wide views of forested hills. The philosopher in him treasured the quiet privacy of a tranquil home.

The year before the fire, Jefferson recorded in his garden book the planting of fruit trees including apples, pears, peaches, figs, walnuts, and pomegranates. A month after the fire he organized paid craftsmen and gangs of slaves, some skilled and others simple laborers, to speed the digging of cellars and the laying of foundations.

Jefferson's study of architecture was as methodical as his study of law. George Wythe probably introduced him to his father-in-law, Richard Taliaferro, a Williamsburg architect and builder. Taliaferro may have shown Jefferson a four-volume work on classical Roman architecture by Andrea Palladio, published in 1570. Jefferson always considered this his architectural bible. By the time he was working on Monticello, he had also studied *Select Architecture* by the English architect Robert Morris, published in 1757. In this book Jefferson found the drawings for a country house that are clearly echoed in the lines of Monticello. The plans called for a two-story central structure housing a front hall, spacious parlor, and two upstairs bedrooms. This was to be flanked, east and west, by two single-story wings, one for the master bedroom, the other for the dining room. Workshops, kitchen, laundry, outhouse, and storehouse would be dug into the slope of the mountain, out of sight but connected to the main house by two roofed corridors. By October 1770, Jefferson was able to move into the tiny one-room brick cottage that had been built on the outer end of the eastern corridor.

In the spring of 1771, Thomas Jefferson began to see a good deal of a pretty and lively twenty-three-year-old widow. He probably met her in Williamsburg, but he often went to see her and her three-year-old son at the house of her father, a plantation called the Forest, not far from Williamsburg. Martha Wayles Skelton was a beautiful woman with hazel eyes and auburn hair. She had many admirers and Jefferson had plenty of competition. Nevertheless, the two had much in common. They loved books and they loved music. In fact, it was music that cemented their relationship. Martha played keyboard instruments exquisitely. At the Forest, she and Thomas often enjoyed playing harpsichord and violin duets. Her other suitors gave up.

That summer, Martha's little boy died. In the fall Jefferson was busy with his law practice and getting himself reelected to the House of Burgesses. In spite of these problems, the courtship continued, and the wedding took place on New Year's Day 1772. The ceremony was performed by two priests of the Church of England, the official religion of the colony of Virginia. The celebration afterward, with dances, parties, food, and wine, went on for over two weeks. Finally, amid snow flurries, Mr. and Mrs. Jefferson set out for Monticello in a phaeton, or light horse-drawn carriage. They had to stop for the night at Tuckahoe but the next day they rode on horseback into what had become a whirling blizzard. Struggling through howling wind and deep drifts, they reached the mountaintop in the middle of the night. Wisely, the slaves had already gone to bed in their cabins. The lovers lit their own fire in the little one-room brick cottage and snuggled down, sur-rounded by stacks of new books. Outside, Jefferson wrote later, was "the deepest snow we have ever seen."

That spring was an unusually hectic one because the melting snows caused the Rivanna River to flood. Soggy ground slowed the progress of building at Monticello but Jefferson found time to super-vise the planting of the various crops. Despite the muddy conditions, he was leading the life he liked best and his beloved Martha, or Patty as her family had nicknamed her, was pregnant. The child was born in the fall, a premature and very sick little girl. They named her Martha and eventually she was nursed to good health by a household slave. Called Patsy in childhood, Martha grew up to be a strong support for her father throughout his life.

Life at Monticello was now more important than ever to Jefferson. In the spring of 1773, he organized the planting of new vegetable gar-dens near the orchards. He and Patty often read to each other and he also spent a great deal of time studying books on history and philoso-phy. Sadly, the happy spell of springtime was broken in May when Dabney Carr died of a mysterious fever. Jefferson brought the six Carr children and their mother, his sister Martha, to live at Monticello. Two weeks later Patty's father died. Jefferson had become fond of his father-in-law even though, at the time of his death, John Wayles was living with one of his female slaves. This was not unusual among Virginia planters but it was a custom Jefferson hated. In addition, although he was on record as being opposed to slavery, he was now responsible for the 135 slaves his wife had inherited. A few of them were the children of John Wayles. Perhaps this was one of the things that encouraged Jefferson, in the spring of 1774, to help set up a company that was to grow olive trees to make oil and grapevines to make wine with the labor of paid workers instead of slaves.

Two of the shareholders in the company would be on opposite sides in the Revolutionary War. They were George Washington, future commander of the Continental Army, and Lord Dunmore, the royal governor of Virginia. Even in 1774, only a year before the first battle of the American Revolution, few people could imagine that the colonies would actually go to war with Great Britain. Nevertheless, a civil war was in the making and taxation was the major issue.

When it finally became clear that the Townshend Acts were failing to produce revenue, Parliament repealed them except for the tax on tea, which was kept as a symbol of Britain's right to tax the colonies. In 1773 an additional Tea Act so incensed Samuel Adams in Boston that he organized a now famous protest. On December 16, a gang disguised as Indians boarded three ships belonging to the British East India Company, smashed over three hundred wooden chests containing ninety thousand pounds of tea, and threw the mess into the harbor. Parliament responded to the Boston Tea Party by passing several acts which became known in the colonies as the Intolerable Acts. One of these, the Boston Port Bill, ordered the seaport closed to all commerce until the tea was paid for. Widespread unemployment might have led to starvation in the streets of Boston if other colonial ports had not sent food.

News of the Boston Port Bill threw colonial legislatures into turmoil. Many people, including some of the radicals, thought the Bostonians' destruction of private property was inexcusable. On the other hand, most felt Parliament's punishment was far too harsh. In Virginia, a secret committee of young burgesses drew up a resolution,

The Boston Tea Party.

probably drafted by Jefferson, to support the "sister colony." It called for a day of fasting and prayer on June 1, 1774, the date the port of Boston was to be closed. Governor Dunmore read the term *sister colony* as treasonous and immediately dissolved the House of Burgesses. As usual, the burgesses reconvened in the Raleigh Tavern. They voted to hold another meeting on August 1 to discuss ways to join other colonies in support of Massachusetts. The possibility of holding an annual continental congress was also mentioned.

Governor Dunmore would have found the agenda of this meeting treasonous, but he was busy preparing for a war with some Indian tribes west of the mountains. White farmers had begun to settle in a part of Virginia that is now the state of Kentucky. This disturbed the Shawnee Indians, who had been led to believe that white settlers would never cross the Appalachian Mountains. Claiming that Virginia's royal charter granted the colony lands stretching from the Atlantic shore to the Pacific Ocean, Dunmore decided to have the Shawnee driven out of Kentucky. The Indians fought back and atrocities were committed on both sides throughout the summer. Without the consent of the legislature, Governor Dunmore called out the Virginia militia and led them west to fight the Indians. In a major battle in the fall he defeated an alliance of Indian tribes led by the Shawnee.

While Dunmore was skirmishing with Indians, Jefferson was at Monticello supervising the cultivation of his fields and drafting a paper to present at the meeting on August 1. On a foundation of his earlier readings in Locke, and his recent readings in history, he was building a statement of rights. "Kings," he wrote, "are the servants, not the proprietors of the people," meaning that George III should be protecting his subjects instead of allowing Parliament to enslave them. In this document Jefferson was not yet suggesting independence. He thought that there could be an honest and reasonable cooperation between the king and the American people. He believed, however, that all people were born naturally entitled to decide how they should be governed. "The God who gave us life," he wrote, "gave us liberty."

On the road to Williamsburg to present his position paper, Jefferson was stricken with dysentery and had to return to Monticello to recover. He sent a copy of the paper to his cousin Peyton Randolph, who was to preside at the meeting. He sent another copy to Patrick Henry in the hope that he would offer it as a resolution at the meeting. Henry never said a word about it. Years later, in his autobiography,

*King George III
of England.*

Jefferson wrote that Henry might have been too lazy to read the paper. It was also possible that even the radical Patrick Henry thought the position a bit too extreme and chose to make no comment. Many people at the convention applauded the spirit of Jefferson's words but were unwilling to completely deny the authority of Parliament. Some of

Jefferson's friends, however, had the document printed and gave it the title *A Summary View of the Rights of British America.* This paper, which Jefferson had intended as a first draft, became a published document and was circulated throughout the colonies. Eventually it was read by authorities in London, who then added Jefferson's name to a growing list of Americans they considered dangerous.

Lying ill at Monticello, Jefferson could not be elected as a delegate to the First Continental Congress at Philadelphia in September 1774. He was, however, present in March 1775 at an illegal gathering of Virginia burgesses held in Richmond. The meeting was called to discuss the recommendations of the Congress of 1774. A main topic was one of Parliament's Intolerable Acts, the Quebec Act, which established laws to govern Canada. In this bill the province of Quebec was defined as stretching from north of the Saint Lawrence River all the way down through territory in the Ohio River Valley, beyond the Appalachian Mountains. It was to be ruled solely by a royal governor appointed by the king. There would be no local legislature, so the taxes would be voted directly by Parliament in London. This scheme would cut off the western lands that other Atlantic colonies, especially Virginia, thought were rightly their own to develop. The colonial legislatures saw it as a major threat because a powerful British authority would be established at their backs. Fear of the Quebec Act and anger over past outrages such as the Stamp Act, the Townshend Acts, and the closing of the port of Boston led the Congress to call for an embargo on goods imported from Great Britain.

Jefferson felt that the First Continental Congress had been too cautious in expressing opposition to England's long history of attempted tyranny. In the meeting at Richmond, the Tidewater burgesses also seemed to favor caution. They hoped to express their objections politely, without offending King George III or Parliament. Patrick Henry, on the other hand, stood up to say it was time to fight. He believed it was disloyal to the other colonies to be so restrained. "Gentlemen may cry, peace, peace," he said, "but there is no peace. The war is actually begun." And bending low like a prisoner in chains, he asked, "Is life so dear or peace so sweet, as to be purchased at the price of chains and slavery?" He then stretched upward, as if breaking his chains. "I know not what course others may take, but as for me," he shouted, while raising an imaginary dagger and plunging it to his chest, "give me liberty or give me death!"

Henry's dramatic speech persuaded just enough conservative burgesses. A vote passed to organize county militias and start planning for the defense of Virginia against British troops. Then delegates were selected for the Second Continental Congress, soon to meet in Philadelphia. Because of growing mob violence in Virginia, it was anticipated that one of the delegates, Peyton Randolph, who was to preside over the Congress, might be called back to Williamsburg to preside over the House of Burgesses. Jefferson was selected as his alternate. He returned to Monticello to supervise the planting of crops and to look after some new horses. Then early in the first week of May, a messenger rode up the mountain with the shocking news that on April 18, British redcoats and Massachusetts militiamen had exchanged shots at Lexington and Concord. In a letter Jefferson wrote, "This accident has cut off our last hopes of reconciliation." Some called it a rebellion, others a revolution. Whatever it was, England and her colonies were now involved in a civil war.

As expected, Peyton Randolph had to hurry back to Williamsburg

The Battle of Concord Bridge.

to preside over an emergency session of the House of Burgesses called by Governor Dunmore for June 1. The purpose was to discuss Parliament's belated proposal to make a reconciliation with the colonies. Jefferson helped write a rejection of the offer, stating, "we viewed it in every point of light . . . and, with pain and disappointment we must ultimately declare it only changes the form of oppression." He then traveled on to take up his responsibility as a delegate to the Continental Congress, which had already been in session for several weeks. He was warmly welcomed in Philadelphia by many delegates who had read his *Summary View of the Rights of British America*. One admirer who was particularly impressed with Jefferson's writing ability was a round and brisk little lawyer from Massachusetts named John Adams. He was a cousin of another delegate, Samuel Adams of Boston.

It was John Adams who first suggested the election of George Washington as commander in chief of the Continental Army. A committee of five, including the aged but still witty Benjamin Franklin of Pennsylvania, was preparing a document called "A Declaration on the Necessity of Taking Up Arms" for Washington to publish when he traveled to a military camp outside Boston. The first draft had been rejected by the Congress when word came from Boston that, in nearby Charlestown, colonial militias had faced British troops in a bloody

John Adams, the lawyer from Massachusetts who suggested that Congress appoint George Washington, from Virginia, to command the Continental Army.

In 1876, a century after the Revolution, Nathaniel Currier and James Merritt Ives of New York published this illustration of George Washington being appointed commander of the Continental Army.

conflict, later called the Battle of Bunker Hill. This news made the need for the declaration more urgent. John Dickinson of Pennsylvania and Thomas Jefferson were added to the committee and Jefferson wrote the next draft. The committee found the language too strong and Dickinson wrote yet another draft that was finally accepted by the Congress after much debate. The whole experience demonstrated how many different points of view were represented in the Continental Congress. Conservatives and radicals had to be extremely patient with each other if they hoped for any sort of cooperation. John

Adams said the Congress was like a convoy of ships. "The fleetest sailors must wait for . . . the slowest."

In the muggy heat of August, Jefferson left Philadelphia to attend another convention in Richmond, where seven delegates for the next Continental Congress were elected, including Peyton Randolph and Thomas Jefferson. On his way back to Monticello, Jefferson stopped to help his cousin John Randolph, Peyton's brother, sell his estate. John Randolph was moving to England because he could not agree with

The Battle of Bunker Hill, first known as the Battle of Charlestown.

the cause of the colonists. On the other hand, his son Edmund was soon appointed as an aide to General Washington. The politics of the times were dividing families and separating friends throughout the colonies. Loyalists were fleeing to Canada, to the Caribbean colonies, or home to England.

Almost as soon as Jefferson returned to Monticello in September, his second daughter, Jane, died. He could not stay very long after the child's funeral, however, as he had to get back to the Continental Congress in October. Shortly after his return to Philadelphia, he was at a dinner party with Peyton Randolph when his cousin died suddenly, probably of a heart attack. Jefferson reported the sad news in a letter to John Randolph in London. In the same letter he wrote, "There is not in the British empire, a man who more cordially loves a union with Great Britain. But by the God who made me, I will cease to exist before I yield to a connection on such terms as the British Parliament propose; and in this I think I speak the sentiments of America." While clearly saying that the colonies would prefer to remain within the empire, Jefferson was also hinting at the possibility of separation from Great Britain. In fact, George III had pushed the colonies closer to that alternative with a royal proclamation stating that the Americans were in rebellion and would be severely punished for the treasonous crime.

In December 1775, Jefferson hurried back to Virginia because he was worried about the safety of his wife and daughter. Patty, who was in poor health, and Patsy were staying with relatives at the former Wayles plantation, the Forest. There was serious fighting around the port of Norfolk. Governor Dunmore had declared martial law and fled with his troops, including runaway slaves, to British ships in the harbor. He then had the town bombarded, and the American militiamen added to the violent confusion by setting fire to buildings owned by Loyalists. Jefferson moved his family back to Monticello in order to keep them as far as possible from the fighting. At the end of March his mother died. This must have been the final item of stress needed to bring on one of Jefferson's painful migraine attacks. For the next month or more he was confined to his bed by devastating headaches.

During his illness Jefferson received from Philadelphia a copy of a pamphlet called *Common Sense* by Thomas Paine, a man who had emigrated from England only two years earlier. The essay was filled with ringing language insisting that the time had come for the American

Thomas Paine, author of Common Sense.

colonies to separate from England. "The period of debate is closed," wrote Paine. "Arms as the last resource decide the contest.... The sun never shined on a cause of greater worth." The idea of independence was spreading through the colonies, especially in Virginia. In fact it was Richard Henry Lee, of the Virginia delegation to the Continental Congress, who on June 7 proposed the resolution that "these United Colonies are, and of right ought to be, free and independent States... and that all political connection between them and the State of Great

Richard Henry Lee of Virginia proposed a resolution in the Continental Congress "that these United Colonies . . . ought to be free and independent States."

Britain is and ought to be, totally dissolved." Jefferson, who had returned to Philadelphia three weeks earlier, listened to the debate that followed the proposal. It became clear that, although the New England colonies were strongly supportive, New York, New Jersey, Pennsylvania, Delaware, Maryland, and South Carolina "were not yet matured," as Jefferson later wrote, "for falling from the parent stem." To give the undecided delegations time to consult with their home constituents, the Congress decided to put off a final vote on the resolution until July 1.

Meanwhile a committee was appointed to compose a declaration explaining the resolution. The members were Roger Sherman of Connecticut, Robert Livingston of New York, Benjamin Franklin, John Adams, and Thomas Jefferson as chairman. Jefferson may have asked Adams to write the first draft. Nearly fifty years later, Adams recalled the reasons he offered to Jefferson for refusing the request. "Reason first: A Virginian ought to appear at the head of this business. Reason second: I am obnoxious . . . and unpopular. Reason third: You can write ten times better than I can."

Jefferson's later recollection was that the committee had unanimously asked him to write the first draft. Every evening for the next two weeks, he trudged up the stairs to his rented rooms and sat down at a small portable desk he had designed, which was built by a Philadelphia cabinetmaker. Here, after hours of committee meetings and debate in Congress, Jefferson labored on a document titled in his autobiography "A DECLARATION BY THE REPRESENTATIVES OF THE UNITED STATES OF AMERICA, IN *GENERAL* CONGRESS ASSEMBLED." It began, "When, in the course of human events, it becomes necessary for one people to dissolve the political bands which have

The Declaration committee with Jefferson as chairman.

connected them with another . . . they should declare the causes which impel them to the separation." Jefferson did not have to consult out-side sources for his words. The concepts of John Locke and other Enlightenment philosophers were like plants rooted deeply in the gar-den of his mind. It came naturally for him to continue with, "We hold these truths to be self evident: That all men are created equal; that they are endowed by their Creator with inherent and inalienable rights; that among these are life, liberty and the pursuit of happiness." Congress later changed the words "inherent and inalienable rights" to "certain inalienable rights," but Jefferson's message remains. These rights should be protected by a government empowered only by the consent of the people who are being governed. "Whenever any form of government becomes destructive of these ends," Jefferson wrote on, "it is the right of the people to alter or abolish it, and to institute new government."

The Natural Bridge of Virginia and surrounding land was purchased by Jefferson in 1775.

CHAPTER FOUR

The State of Virginia

On July 2, 1776, the Continental Congress voted in favor of Richard Henry Lee's June 7 resolution for independence. Then for three days they debated the exact wording of the declaration written to justify it. Jefferson listened in unhappy silence. Once, Ben Franklin tried to cheer him up by whispering a ridiculous tale about a hatter who had designed a signboard for his business. "John Thompson, hatter, makes and sells hats for ready money" were to be the words above a picture of a hat. When Thompson then asked his friends for suggestions, one said the word "hatter" was redundant. Another wanted to eliminate "makes" because people would not care who actually made the hats. A third said that "for ready money" was unnecessary as customers were not being offered credit. Others said the word "sells" was not needed as no one expected the hats to be given away and the word "hat" was useless next to the image of a hat. The final sign displayed the name "John Thompson" over a painting of a hat. Although he listened politely to Franklin's story, Jefferson was not amused. As it turned out, his writing was edited somewhat less harshly than the hatter's. Late in the evening of July 4, Congress voted to adopt a document that, in spite of significant changes, was still Jefferson's own composition.

When the sheriff of Philadelphia County read it aloud on July 8, the cheering crowd outside what is now called Independence Hall had no idea who had written it. A number of the original phrases had been

Jefferson and the committee presenting the Declaration of Independence in the Continental Congress.

revised and some passages were cut out entirely. Jefferson was especially disappointed that his condemnation of slavery had been removed. In the list of accusations against George III he had written that the king had "waged a cruel war against . . . a distant people who never offended him, captivating them and carrying them into slavery in another hemisphere, or to incur a miserable death in their transportation hither." In addition, Jefferson had condemned the king for "suppressing every legislative attempt to prohibit . . . this execrable commerce . . . a market where men should be bought and sold." Congressional delegates from Georgia and South Carolina, where the plantation economy was dependent on slave labor, insisted on the elimination of the references to slavery. Other delegates from New England, where maritime businessmen had become wealthy in the slave trade, agreed with the southerners.

Jefferson felt his work in Philadelphia was done. Now the old colonies needed to be shaped into new countries. To Jefferson it seemed far more important to participate in establishing a sound form of government in what he regarded as his own country, Virginia. Furthermore, he had received news that his wife, Patty, was ill again. He had good reasons to go home, and his term as a delegate to the Continental Congress expired in August. He did not want another term but the Virginia Convention reelected him, and he was forced to stay at least for the rest of the summer. This meant that he was among the fifty-five delegates who finally gathered on August 2 to sign the official Declaration of Independence that Congress had ordered engrossed, or written in formal calligraphy, on durable parchment. The document of July 4 had been signed only by John Hancock, president of the Congress, and Charles Thompson, secretary.

When Richard Henry Lee, who had been absent, returned on September 3 to fill out the Virginia delegation, Jefferson was at last able to go home. He spent three quiet weeks at Monticello and then moved the whole family to George Wythe's house in Williamsburg. The Virginia General Assembly, meeting in the chamber where the burgesses had once met, faced the enormous task of creating a new system of government for the Commonwealth of Virginia. Jefferson saw this as such an important job that he reluctantly declined a request from the Continental Congress to join a commission traveling to France for the purpose of negotiating new business and military agreements. Virginia, the largest of the former colonies, was developing a government that could become a model for many others. Jefferson thought the project was urgent because the fervently unified spirit created by the ongoing war would dwindle in people's hearts as the flames of war died down. Now was the time to generate a strong spirit of reform so that a fair and honest constitution would later be in place to safeguard the rights currently being fought for.

Originally there were five men chosen for the Committee to Revise the Laws of the Commonwealth. Two of them, who were not in the best of health anyway, decided they were unqualified for the legal work and resigned. This left the monumental task to three men, Edmund Pendleton, George Wythe, and Jefferson, who, at thirty-three, was by far the youngest. He was also the most active. Between 1776 and 1779, both at Monticello and in Williamsburg, he worked harder than at any other time in his life. He had numerous legislative goals in mind and reached for them all at the same time. Four were especially important. The first was to reduce the dominance of the Tidewater aristocrats by eliminating the law of primogeniture and increasing the number of people allowed to vote. The second was to establish freedom of religion for the growing number of non-Anglican Virginians—Lutherans, Presbyterians, Quakers, and Baptists—by eliminating the Church of England as the government-supported religion of the commonwealth. The third was to work toward the gradual abolition of slavery. The fourth was to establish some form of free public education. All four of these goals were intended to lead Virginia toward a society where people would have the self-respect and the knowledge to participate in their own government.

It would have been impossible to achieve these goals immediately and completely. Jefferson knew that if his legislative efforts appeared too radical, they would be defeated by the conservatives in the Virginia Assembly. Avoiding outright confrontation, he and a new friend, James Madison, introduced one bill at a time in efforts to establish principles of law that could be improved and refined over many years, perhaps long after both men had left the scene. The two were a natural team. Like Jefferson at William and Mary, Madison had been influenced by Enlightenment concepts at Princeton, then called the College of New Jersey. They believed in similar goals for government, and each man's personality complemented the other's. Jefferson envisioned legislative concepts and Madison studied practical ways to make them into law. Following their step-at-a-time strategy, Jefferson introduced several different resolutions aimed at freedom of religion. The only one that passed was the exemption of non-Anglicans from taxes to support the Church of England in Virginia, but the seed was planted. Ten years later, the assembly enacted the Statute of Virginia for Religious Freedom. Jefferson came to regard this as one of the three most significant achievements of his life.

James Madison, Jefferson's friend and colleague in revising the laws of the Commonwealth of Virginia.

Rather than play legislative politics, Jefferson would have preferred to retire permanently to Monticello. Patty was in poor health following the birth of their son on May 28, 1777. The baby was sickly and died less than three weeks later with no recorded name. Aside from wishing to be with his family, Jefferson enjoyed the building and farming work at Monticello. Furthermore, it was a quiet place, where he could study legal history and write the proposals for judicial reform. These problems and distractions, plus the birth of his daughter Mary, nicknamed Polly, on August 1, 1778, might explain why he missed so many meetings of the legislative session that fall. Twice he was taken into custody by the assembly's sergeant-at-arms and had to pay fines. In spite of his absences, his colleagues appreciated his hard research and paperwork. On June 1, 1779, the two houses of the General Assembly elected Thomas Jefferson to a one-year term as governor of Virginia.

There had been two other strong candidates, John Page and Thomas Nelson Jr. Nevertheless, the election demonstrated that Jefferson was admired by his fellow legislators for his knowledge of law and history. He was also deeply respected for his nonpartisan attitude toward legislation. In a time of peace, the office would have been an honor, but now there was a war going on. Even if he had not been inclined toward pacifism, Jefferson's nonmilitary mind made it hard for him to be a strong wartime leader. Furthermore, the office of governor was not a position of power. According to the new state constitution, the governor held the responsibility of carrying out the laws of the commonwealth. All his executive actions, however, required the approval of the Council of State, a group of eight elected from the General Assembly. The legislature had all the authority that might have been useful to the executive in time of war. The governor was a figurehead, permitted to serve only a year at a time, for up to three terms.

Until Jefferson's election, the battles of the Revolution had been fought either north or south of Virginia. Most of the soldiers recruited in Virginia were now with George Washington in the Continental Army, which, in 1777-78, had suffered through a bitter winter at Valley Forge in Pennsylvania. Other Virginia militias had been sent by Governor Patrick Henry in 1778 on a secret mission to take the Old Northwest lands south of the Great Lakes from the British. They remained in the Illinois Territory for two years. By the time Jefferson moved into the Governor's Palace in Williamsburg in 1779, the British had blockaded Chesapeake Bay, choking off commerce and smothering Virginia's economy. Many counties were unable to pay their taxes, and the government of Virginia became stalled with no money, no soldiers, and almost no leadership. At first, Jefferson devised creative ways to adapt to the unforeseen difficulties. Through James Madison, his staunch supporter on the council, he was able to manage the council and make the government somewhat more efficient. Also, because British ships could sail in from Chesapeake Bay to attack Williamsburg, Jefferson decided to move the capital farther inland to Richmond. This had the additional advantage of making the capital more accessible to frontier people from the Piedmont and thus weakening the power of the Tidewater aristocracy.

The war finally came to the commonwealth in 1780. Continental Army troops that had been fighting in the Carolinas retreated north into Virginia in August. In October a British fleet appeared in the Chesapeake and landed five thousand troops at Newport News. Governor Jefferson set aside his philosophical opposition to strong governmental power and asked the Council of State to reinforce the shaky county militias by establishing a regular Army of Virginia. The council refused to authorize raising a state army and the defenses of the commonwealth remained weak.

On January 2, 1781, Jefferson was informed that British ships had sailed up the James River. He assumed they were only bringing troops to attack Williamsburg. He failed to understand the seriousness of the military threat until he was awakened before dawn on January 4 by a messenger with alarming news. The turncoat Brigadier General Benedict Arnold was leading a thousand infantrymen farther up the river to capture Richmond and the governor himself. Jefferson had already sent his family up the river to Tuckahoe. Now he and the Council of State along with two hundred militiamen fled Richmond just before Arnold marched in. Hastily, Jefferson took his family to a safer place

Benedict Arnold, a hero of the American Revolution until he went over to the British side in 1780.

across the river from Tuckahoe and then galloped back to Westham, near Richmond, to manage the frantic evacuation of military supplies. He rode back and forth in rain and snow until his horse collapsed and he had to borrow another. Meanwhile, Arnold sent troops up to Westham to destroy the cannon foundry there and dump three hundred barrels of gunpowder into the river.

On April 15, Jefferson's infant daughter, Lucy, born the previous November, died. After the funeral, the family moved back to Monticello. Jefferson tried to re-establish the last shreds of the government in nearby Charlottesville, but most of the councilors had gone home to their own plantations. A French major general, the marquis de

Lafayette, was sent by Washington, with a few troops from the Continental Army, to help defend Virginia. It was the beginning of a lifelong friendship, despite the fact that Jefferson was unable to respond to Lafayette's request that the Virginia county militias be ordered to reinforce his small detachment. A discouraged Jefferson had to explain that legally he was not permitted to call up the militia without a vote of approval from the Council of State, most of whom were unavailable. Then Lafayette was driven northward by the troops of Lord

The marquis de Lafayette, a major general under Washington.

Cornwallis, second in command of the British forces in America. On June 1, the last day of his second term, Governor Jefferson resigned. Bitter, depressed, and extremely tired, he had earlier decided he would not consider a third term. In a letter to the assembly, he suggested that General Thomas Nelson, commander of the state militia, be made governor in order to consolidate "civil and military power in the same hands."

Two days earlier, Cornwallis had ordered that a detachment of dragoons be sent to Charlottesville under Colonel Banastre Tarleton to capture members of the assembly and Governor Jefferson. On Sunday

Lord Cornwallis, second in command of British troops in America.

Colonel Banastre Tarleton, sent by Cornwallis to capture members of the Virginia Assembly and Governor Jefferson.

June 3, they started out, moving rapidly and riding through the night. Tarleton hoped to make the raid a complete surprise. He would have succeeded except for a huge and colorful man named Captain Jack Jouett, who happened to be at a tavern where the dragoons made a stop forty miles from Charlottesville. Jouett rode feverishly through the backwoods and arrived at Monticello before dawn. Jefferson then packed his wife, their daughters, Patsy and Polly, plus two slaves into a

Captain Jack Jouett, who saved Jefferson from being captured.

carriage and sent them to a house on a neighboring mountain. He remained to see to the safe departure of some houseguests and his other slaves. He himself did not leave Monticello until he saw Tarleton's men through his spyglass.

Jefferson's unwillingness to face two hundred and fifty British soldiers alone was considered cowardice by some of his fellow Virginians. They also blamed him for allowing the commonwealth to be humiliated by military disasters. The government of Virginia was in chaos, and the General Assembly was not able to elect the new governor, Thomas Nelson, until it met at Staunton on June 12. Then, after voting to award Captain Jouett a sword and a pair of pistols, a resolution was passed that "an inquiry be made into the conduct of the Executive of this State for the last twelve months." Jefferson was sure that Patrick Henry was behind the resolution and afterward felt nothing but contempt for his former friend. To Jefferson, it would always seem the most dismal period of his public career, but the investigation fizzled as no one came forward to offer evidence or information. On October 17, 1781, Cornwallis surrendered to American and French forces at Yorktown, Virginia, and the war was over. In December the assembly voted to thank Jefferson for his services as governor and dismiss the rumors that had led to the inquiry.

After the flight from Monticello, the Jefferson family had moved even farther away to a plantation called Poplar Forest that was part of Patty's inheritance. On a morning ride, Jefferson was thrown from his horse and broke his left wrist. Since his arm was in a sling he could not ride, so he finished writing a work, not intended for publication, called *Notes on the State of Virginia.* He had begun it in October 1780 as a response to a questionnaire sent to each state governor by a French diplomat named François Barbé-Marbois. It was an organized presentation based on the huge piles of notes Jefferson had collected over the years on the geography, climate, natural history, agriculture, population, laws, religion, commerce, customs, and political history of Virginia. Jefferson the scientist, listing all the known species of birds in the state, collaborated with Jefferson the artist, painting a verbal landscape of the Natural Bridge, which he had bought in 1775. "So beautiful an arch," wrote Jefferson, "so elevated, so light, and springing, as it were, up to heaven, the rapture of the spectator is really indescribable!" The book is both an encyclopedia and a work of literature.

Notes on the State of Virginia is a remarkable achievement, but modern readers will find one particularly offensive passage. Although Jefferson wrote about Indians with admiration, stating that they were the intellectual equals of white men, he was not so glowing about

The Natural Bridge described poetically by Jefferson in
Notes on the State of Virginia.

African-Americans. The same man who wrote "all men are created equal" also wrote of blacks "that in memory they are equal to whites; in reason much inferior . . . and that in imagination they are dull." He admitted that it would be "right to make great allowances for the difference of condition, of education . . . of the sphere in which they move." He did not, however, make nearly enough allowance. Evidently, it did not occur to him that Indians were born free to grow up in the traditions of their own tribes, but blacks were from many different African traditions. Furthermore, whether born in Africa or America, they were all forced to live at the bottom level of a society that was not their own heritage.

Living at the top level of a slave-owning society, Jefferson could not experience its harshest realities, but he was not entirely blind to the cruel injustice of the system. Elsewhere in his *Notes* he observed, "The whole commerce between master and slave is a perpetual exercise of . . . unremitting despotism on the one part, and degrading submission on the other. Our children see this, and learn to imitate it." He went on to express his fear that this contradiction of the new nation's basic liberties had to lead to trouble. "I tremble for my country when I reflect that God is just: that his justice cannot sleep forever." Jefferson feared that the "deep rooted prejudices entertained by the whites; the thousand recollections, by the blacks of the injuries they have sustained . . . will divide us into parties, and produce convulsions which will probably never end but in the extermination of one or the other race." The Civil War of the nineteenth century and the civil rights struggle of the twentieth were yet to come. Jefferson was writing in the eighteenth century.

In order to avoid a racial holocaust, Jefferson outlined a long-term plan to educate younger blacks at public expense until the women were eighteen and the men twenty-one. They could then be relocated elsewhere, perhaps back to Africa, in self-supporting communities of their own. The concept may seem hopelessly impractical today, but at the time, there were others who thought along the same lines. Paul Cuffe, a free black Quaker in Dartmouth, Massachusetts, felt that returning to Africa was a good idea. In 1815, Cuffe, who was a wealthy merchant, sailed on one of his own ships with a group of thirty-eight blacks to Sierra Leone in Africa, where he intended to establish a free black community. His plan died with him in 1817, but in 1822, just south of Sierra Leone, a colony of freed slaves was established in what is now the independent country of Liberia.

It is astonishing that the first draft of *Notes on the State of Virginia* was written at all, as it was composed during a period when its author's public career was in turmoil. No matter how flawed the work may seem now, it must be recognized as the creation of a clear-minded and visionary writer. For example, in describing his excavation of an Indian burial mound, Jefferson outlines an archaeological method that was a century ahead of its time. His theories on principles of architecture are still admired by professional architects. His commentaries on history and politics are always perceptive and his observations on agriculture are given in painstaking detail.

When Jefferson returned to Monticello in 1781 his intention was to settle down to life at home with Patty, their two daughters, and his sister Martha Carr with her six children. It was not just an idyllic country retirement. Although Tarleton had left Monticello in fairly good order, Cornwallis's troops had devastated Jefferson's other lands, destroying crops, carrying off livestock, and leading away about thirty

Although his troops devastated parts of Virginia, Cornwallis later retreated down the Yorktown peninsula, where Washington's army forced him to surrender on October 19, 1781.

slaves, most of whom died of smallpox and fever in the army camp. Things had to be put back in order and he felt he could not respond to the requests of his friends in the General Assembly that he return to public life. Like most of his contemporaries, Jefferson believed he had an obligation to serve a part of his life in public service. He had, however, served many years in several offices, and as he wrote to his young friend and law student James Monroe, he did not think "the state has a *perpetual* right to the services of all its members."

There was a more urgent reason for Jefferson to stay home. On May 8, 1782, Patty gave birth to a daughter who was named Lucy Elizabeth, after the baby who had died the year before. Following the difficult birth, Patty remained extremely ill. For four months, Jefferson and his sister Martha took turns nursing her. According to several household slaves who were present at the end, Patty said she did not want her children to have a stepmother and Jefferson promised her he would never marry again. When she finally slipped into a coma, he fainted and had to be carried from the room. On September 6, 1782, Jefferson wrote in his account book, "My dear wife died this day at 11:45 a.m." He stayed in his library for three weeks, pacing day and night. When he reappeared, his only activity was riding horseback day after day in the woods, accompanied by his ten-year-old daughter, Patsy. "In those melancholy rambles," she wrote years later, "I was his constant companion, a solitary witness to many a violent burst of grief."

Jefferson with a bust of Franklin. Jefferson succeeded Franklin as American minister to France.

CHAPTER FIVE

The Old World and the New Nation

A letter from Philadelphia offering a trip to France pulled Jefferson from what he called the "stupor of mind" that had been brought on by the death of his wife. Congress, acting on a motion by James Madison, had voted to send him to Paris to help John Adams and Benjamin Franklin negotiate the peace agreement with Great Britain. He wrote a letter of acceptance the next day. As soon as he could take care of his responsibilities in Virginia, he and young Patsy traveled first to Philadelphia and then south to Baltimore, where a French ship was supposed to be waiting for them. Unfortunately, it was waiting frozen in winter ice. Furthermore, even though Cornwallis had surrendered at Yorktown the year before, there were still twenty-five hostile British warships cruising just outside Chesapeake Bay. Jefferson asked Congress for further instructions, but by the time everything got sorted out, negotiations in Paris had progressed to a point where he was no longer needed.

During the boring wait in Baltimore, Jefferson worried about how the new nation was developing. Now that the authority of Great Britain had been thrown off, he feared that the individual states would start to fight with one another because they lacked a form of government that could unify them. By the time he and Patsy returned to Monticello, he had concluded that Virginia's backwoods, Piedmont, and Tidewater factions faced a similar danger. In a revision of *Notes on the State of Virginia* for future publication, Jefferson included a plan for a new Virginia constitution. He envisioned a strong government but one that did not concentrate power in just one authority. "The powers of government shall be divided into three distinct departments," he wrote, "those which are legislative . . . those which are judiciary . . . and those which are executive." No doubt recalling how his power as governor had been severely limited by the Council of State elected from the legislature, Jefferson now proposed to keep the three powers clearly separate. "No person, or collection of persons . . . shall exercise any power properly belonging to either of the others." Jefferson's model foreshadowed many later constitutions around the world, beginning with the United States Constitution, which would be framed in 1787.

In June 1783, Madison started a successful campaign to get Jefferson elected to the Virginia delegation to the Continental Congress that was to meet on November 1. When he and Patsy arrived in Philadelphia, the Congress had moved to Princeton, New Jersey, to avoid a confrontation with angry soldiers demanding back pay. Jefferson left Patsy in Philadelphia with arrangements for a course of study in literature and science that was much more rigorous than what was normally expected of girls at the time. Explaining this in a letter to his friend Barbé-Marbois he wrote, "The chance that in marriage she will draw a blockhead I calculate at about fourteen to one."

He wanted to make sure that, no matter who Patsy's future husband might be, she would see to it her children got the best education.

As soon as Jefferson got to Princeton, the Congress, under pressure to find a more central location, decided to move to Annapolis, Maryland. With Congress finally in session, Jefferson became chairman of the Committee for the Ratification of the Treaty of Paris, the peace agreement between the United States and Great Britain. One of the items in this treaty, the cession of the Old Northwest to the former colonies, nearly doubled the size of the new nation. Although Virginia had already taken possession of these lands between the Ohio and Mississippi Rivers during the Revolution, Connecticut, New York,

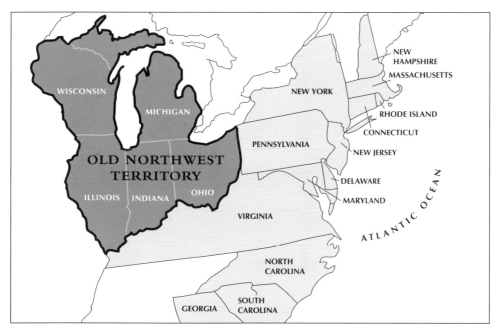

The Old Northwest Territory eventually became the states of Wisconsin, Illinois, Michigan, Indiana, and Ohio.

and Massachusetts had conflicting claims in the same area. Jefferson devised a plan for all parties to give up their claims. The United States government would then manage the western lands as fourteen territories. Each would become a new state when its population reached twenty thousand. Although Jefferson's proposals later served as the basis for a land management plan called the Northwest Ordinance, they now became bogged down in debate. Congress did not care for most of the state names he suggested, such as Assenisipia and Cherroesus, but in modified forms Michigania and Illinoia survived.

Another of Jefferson's proposals for the western lands stated that after 1800 there should be no slavery in the new states. This idea provoked a stormy debate and was defeated by one vote. In a letter to a French friend Jefferson wrote, "The voice of a single individual would have prevented this abominable crime from spreading itself over the new country."

There were many other legislative concerns before Congress and Jefferson seemed to be involved in nearly all of them. One of the issues he dealt with was the problem of a national currency. Each state had its own currency. In addition, the coins of England, Spain, France, Portugal, and Holland were also in circulation. Robert Morris, a Philadelphia financier, proposed replacing the chaotic coinage with a complex scheme for a unified national currency. Jefferson thought the system too complicated for daily commerce and offered a simplified proposal he had been contemplating since 1776. Later adopted by Congress, it was the world's first decimal currency. The basic unit was derived from a familiar and widely circulated Spanish silver coin called a dollar.

Jefferson was so busy with various issues in Congress in 1783 and

1784 that he had little social life and it is no wonder that he was frequently laid low by painful migraine headaches. In May 1784, he must have been somewhat relieved to accept Congress's appointment as a commissioner to join John Adams and Benjamin Franklin in Paris to negotiate trade agreements with twenty European countries. Jefferson believed that the economic strength of the country was in agriculture rather than manufacturing, but he felt that he needed to know more about the industry of the northern states if he was to represent their

Benjamin Franklin (left) was popular at the French court. John Adams (right) later became the American minister to Great Britain.

interests in Europe. He picked up Patsy in Philadelphia and started a whirlwind tour that included New York, Connecticut, Rhode Island, Massachusetts, and New Hampshire. On his way through New Haven he met with the president of Yale, Ezra Stiles, who wrote in his diary, "The Governor is a most ingenious naturalist and philosopher, a truly learned and scientific man." At last, with his daughter Patsy, his secretary and law student William Short, and a slave named James Hemings, Jefferson sailed from Boston. They landed in England, crossed the English Channel, toured the quiet countryside of northern France, and arrived in Paris on August 6, 1784, riding in a carriage on the broad Champs-Élysées.

Ezra Stiles, president of Yale, admired Jefferson's learning.

With the help of his friend, François Jean, marquis de Chastellux, who had fought in the American Revolution and visited Monticello, Jefferson enrolled Patsy in the fashionable convent school at the Abbaye Royale de Panthémont. He chose it because it offered an excellent education. As a Protestant who could read French but did not speak it well, Patsy was at first a bit unhappy, but she soon made friends, became popular, and was nicknamed "Jeffy." Probably her new companions were able to offer some comfort when, on one of his frequent visits, her father brought the sad news that her little sister Lucy had died at home in Virginia. In January 1785, Lafayette had brought letters from America informing Jefferson that the previous autumn both Lucy and Polly had come down with serious cases of whooping cough, but Polly had recovered.

Before the grim letters arrived, Jefferson was kept busy establishing a home in Paris and spending his spare time attending concerts, browsing in bookshops, and watching launchings of hot-air balloons in the Tuileries garden. He also spent a lot of time in conference with his old colleagues Adams and Franklin preparing for trade negotiations to eliminate the young nation's economic dependence on British commerce. Then the three emissaries had to present themselves formally at the court of Louis XVI in his splendid palace at Versailles. Diplomacy was a slow and frustrating business. Years later, Jefferson described it in his autobiography. "We sounded the ministers of several European nations, at the court of Versailles," he wrote. "They were ignorant of our commerce, which had always been monopolized by England, and . . . were inclined, therefore, to stand aloof." Most European nations seemed uninterested in making trade agreements with a country founded on rebellion. The Americans did manage some negotiations

A Parisian scene of the 1780s.

with Denmark and the Italian principality of Tuscany, but Frederick the Great, king of Prussia, was the only person who truly recognized the potential of the new nation. He was the first to agree to Jefferson's model treaty of commerce and friendship.

In June 1785, John Adams went to London as the ambassador to England, and in July, eighty-year-old Benjamin Franklin, severely crippled by gout and gallstones, returned to the United States. Thomas Jefferson, newly appointed American minister to France, remained in Paris. When he appeared at the French court, his clothes, although elegantly tailored, were not nearly as splendid as the attire of most diplo-

Frederick the Great of Prussia.

mats, and he did not display any sparkling decorations or gleaming medals. Living quarters, however, were a different matter. Jefferson began hunting for a place that could serve as his official residence and the American embassy. Finally, he rented a magnificent villa on the Champs-Élysées called the Hôtel de Langéac. It had ample stables and beautiful grounds, and Jefferson immediately planned gardens where he would grow American specialties such as corn, sweet potatoes, and watermelons.

The new ambassador's first diplomatic problem was presented by the Barbary States of Morocco, Algeria, Tunisia, and Tripoli on the North African coast. For many years, European nations carrying on trade in the Mediterranean had paid tribute in either goods or cash to these Muslim countries. Intending to force the United States to pay similar tribute, Moroccan ships captured an American vessel, enslaved the crew, and demanded ransom. Twenty-five years later, in his autobiography, Jefferson wrote, "I was very unwilling that we should acquiesce in the European humiliation, of paying a tribute to those lawless pirates." He contacted a number of other ambassadors in Paris and suggested forming a combined naval force to protect commerce. Some countries did not want to alter their agreements with the Barbary States. Others were not sure they could supply the necessary warships. Nevertheless, with the help of the Spanish ambassador to France, Jefferson was able to negotiate a treaty with Morocco to free the American sailors. Although he mistrusted strong central government and national military forces, Jefferson bent his principles enough to suggest creating a United States naval force to punish the Barbary States. John Adams, on the other hand, thought it would be cheaper to pay the ransom than fight. Congress would not agree to either concept and so the Barbary pirates continued to be a nuisance.

American commerce was Jefferson's primary responsibility in Paris, but he found time to welcome a variety of visitors to the Hôtel de Langéac, such as American sailors, French noblemen, and other ambassadors. In the winter of 1786 one of these visitors was explorer John Ledyard of Connecticut, who wanted to set up a company to carry furs from the Pacific Northwest to trade in China. Jefferson, always intensely interested in the unknown lands west of the

Mississippi, encouraged Ledyard's plan to trek east across Siberia, sail from Kamchatka to the Canadian northwest, and from there set out to explore the American West. The trip required the permission of Catherine the Great, empress and czarina of Russia. She refused, but Ledyard went anyway and managed to cross Siberia before he was arrested and brought back to Europe. Although he had not achieved his original goal, Ledyard later wrote to Jefferson that the trip was still worthwhile because he had discovered that Mongolian tribes and American Indians were the same race.

Catherine the Great, empress and czarina of Russia.

In the spring of 1786, Jefferson, at the urgent request of John Adams, went to London to help negotiate a series of trade treaties. While he was in England he took the opportunity to learn all he could about advances in science, particularly the new use of steam power in factories. With Adams, Jefferson also toured the great English country mansions and made notes on the gardens and architecture, including features he would later use at Monticello. Nevertheless, Jefferson did not feel at home in England and felt sure he had been snubbed by King George III when Adams presented him at court.

By contrast, when he returned to Paris, Jefferson found he was much admired. His *Notes on the State of Virginia,* which had been printed first in English and then in a rather bad French translation, had received favorable notice. Earlier he had given a copy of *Notes,* along with a large panther skin he had bought in Philadelphia, to the famous Enlightenment naturalist Georges Louis Leclerc, comte de Buffon. Jefferson had offered the huge hide as proof that Buffon was mistaken in his theory that animals in the New World were degenerate and therefore smaller than European species, but the eminent scientist was not convinced. Later, Jefferson received a shipment of the skeleton and hide of a moose that he had requested from General John Sullivan, governor of New Hampshire. He was upset that the order had cost him well over forty English pounds, but the seven-foot-tall beast persuaded Buffon that his theory was wrong. Jefferson's intellectual reputation was even further enhanced when his Statute of Virginia for Religious Freedom, printed in English, French, and Italian, was highly praised by many scholars and philosophers. He was becoming a celebrity in the cultural center of the Western world.

The magnificent social carousel of Paris took on fresh color for

Jefferson the day he met an Italian-born, blond-haired, blue-eyed musician and painter from England named Maria Cosway. She composed charming pieces for the harp and harpsichord, wrote songs in Italian, and painted pictures that were exhibited at the Royal Academy of Arts in London. But to her husband, the small and foppish painter Richard Cosway, she was merely a pretty little ornament in his extravagant and bawdy life. The mismatched couple were friends of John

Maria Cosway,
a self-portrait.

Trumbull, a painter from Connecticut. Trumbull was in Paris to make sketches for a portrait of Jefferson to be included in a historical painting of the presentation of the Declaration of Independence to Congress. Late in the summer of 1786, he and Jefferson made a trip to study the architectural details of a new building called the Halle aux Bleds, a huge domed indoor market. Earlier, when Trumbull invited the Cosways to join them there, he had no idea that the meeting

The Halle aux Bleds, the indoor Parisian market where Jefferson first met Maria Cosway.

would have a romantic and bittersweet effect on the life of his new friend Jefferson.

All four in the group had previous appointments for the evening but they sent out messengers with excuses and apologies. After dinner at an elegant restaurant in a beautiful park, they went on to a fireworks display in a public garden near Montmartre. For Jefferson, the enchantment lasted long after that evening as the foursome went on cultural excursions almost every day. Finally, Trumbull had to travel on to Germany, and Cosway began the commission for which he had come to Paris, painting miniature portraits of the children of the duc d'Orléans. Jefferson and Maria continued the visits to museums and galleries around town. As the relationship grew, their outings became more intimate, perhaps a picnic in the peaceful garden of a suburban chateau or a leisurely stroll along the river Seine. The tall, plainly dressed Virginian and the petite, Italian-educated Englishwoman made an unusual couple amid the artificial glitter of Paris.

On September 18, Jefferson fell and injured his right wrist. He called the incident "one of those follies" and he never told how it happened. One story was that while rushing to his carriage for a visit to Maria, Jefferson leapt a small fountain in the courtyard of the Hôtel de Langéac and crashed to the pavement. The pain was excruciating but he got into the carriage and went on to see Maria with his wrist wrapped to hide the swelling. The couple's day trip was cut short when Jefferson had to go home in agony and summon a doctor. Two surgeons diagnosed the injury as a bad dislocation but in fact it was a compound fracture.

A different story went around the salons of Paris that Jefferson had hurt himself showing off to Maria by jumping over a fence. Regardless of gossip, the romantic idyll was coming to an end. Jefferson was laid up for two weeks and Maria came to see him several times. On October 4, while they went for a carriage ride around Paris, Maria gave him the depressing news that she and her husband were going back to London. On the day Jefferson went to see them off, he returned to the Hôtel de Langéac in a dismal mood. He spent the next five days writing a long letter to Maria with his left hand. "My Head and My Heart," as it has come to be known, is an elaborate dialogue between reason and emotion that begins with the head scolding the heart: "This is one of the scrapes into which you are ever leading us. You confess your follies, indeed: but still you hug and cherish them." The heart replies that now, amid the pain of grief, is no time for reprimands and tries to shift the blame to the head by saying, "It was you, remember, and not I who desired the meeting . . . I never trouble myself with domes nor arches. . . . The Halle aux Bleds might have rotted down before I should have gone to see it." But the head refuses to be drawn into the silly game and replies, "I reminded you of the follies of the first day. . . . I often told you that you were imprudently engaging your affections under circumstances that must cost you a great deal of pain." Finally, Jefferson, usually the voice of reason, seems to give the last word to the heart: "I feel more fit for death than life. But when I look back on the pleasures of which it is the consequence, I am conscious they are worth the price I am paying."

Despite the emotional pain in his heart and the physical pain in his wrist, Jefferson still had his job to do. In a letter to U.S. Secretary of Foreign Affairs John Jay, he wrote that, to survive economically, the United States had to establish new markets for American goods in Europe. A knowledge of the existing industry and agriculture was essential if Americans hoped to compete in European commerce. An unobtrusive exploratory trip would lay the groundwork for this knowledge.

Leaving William Short in charge of affairs at the Hôtel de Langéac, Jefferson set out on a three-month journey through southern France and Italy, traveling incognito. He first visited the wine country of Champagne and Burgundy. Then he continued through the vineyards and farms in the valley of the Rhone River. Jefferson also studied ancient Roman ruins along the way. In the city of Nîmes he saw a Roman temple called the Maison Carrée that would become a model for the Virginia capitol in Richmond. He wrote to Lafayette's aunt Madame de Tessé, describing himself as "gazing whole hours at the Maison Carrée like a lover at his mistress." Guessing that his words would become gossip at the French court, Jefferson sent the letter to hide his real reason for coming to Nîmes. Five months earlier Dr. José Barbalho da Maia, a Brazilian studying in France, had requested a secret meeting. It turned out that Barbalho wanted the United States to supply military aid to Brazil's rebellion against Portugal. Jefferson said he did not have the official authority to guarantee such support but made it clear that he personally approved of a colony rebelling against a European master.

Jefferson went on to Aix-en-Provence, Marseilles, Nice, and then into northern Italy. Along the way he studied the cultivation of olives, almonds, and oranges, all of which he hoped could be grown in South Carolina and Georgia. He wrote to Maria Cosway in London, describing the spectacular scenery and insisting she paint it. In Lombardy he investigated the production of upland rice and even smuggled out seeds. He hoped Lombard rice could be cultivated on high ground in

Top: The Maison Carrée, a Roman ruin that Jefferson saw at Nîmes.
Bottom: The Virginia State Capitol, modeled after the Maison Carrée.

the Carolinas without the need of swampy country or the slave labor that confined the cultivation of Carolina rice to steamy coastal regions. In side trips around Milan, Jefferson toured dairies to observe the process of making Parmesan cheese. He also learned how to make ice cream. After first traveling farther south in Italy, Jefferson went back to France, studied the canal system in the south, then traveled through the vineyards of Bordeaux and returned to Paris in June by way of the beautiful Loire Valley.

Back in Paris, Jefferson was immediately swamped with work. The first letter he answered, however, was one from Maria Cosway. He wanted to know when the Cosways would visit Paris, but when Maria finally came by herself, they hardly had time for each other. Possibly, Maria was no longer as serious about the relationship as Jefferson. In any case, she had many old friends to see and was swept into a breathless social whirl. Jefferson, on the other hand, was caught up in endless diplomatic details created by American politics. Family matters also began to require more of his time. After a six-week Atlantic crossing, ten-year-old Polly had arrived at the Adamses' house in London and was soon to come to Paris. Jefferson had sent clear instructions to America that his daughter should be accompanied by a responsible adult. As it turned out, her companion for the long voyage was a fourteen-year-old slave girl named Sally Hemings, the young sister of Jefferson's servant James. John Adams's wife Abigail was shocked and wrote to Jefferson that Polly's servant was "wholly incapable of looking . . . after her." Polly had not wanted to come to Paris at all but she soon settled in at the convent school with her older sister, Patsy, and the two shared happy musical weekends with their father.

Shortly before Jefferson returned to Paris from his travels in Italy and southern France, a federal constitutional convention was called to meet in Philadelphia to revise the Articles of Confederation. Since 1781, this document had defined how the United States were to be governed, but it had proved to be ineffective because the central government did not have enough authority. Article 2 provided that each state should retain its sovereign independence. This made it difficult to collect taxes to pay foreign debts, and the so-called "league of friend-

Lydia Smith Russell painted this portrait of Abigail Adams, who, for her time, was an unusually well read woman.

ship" could not easily act as one nation in dealing with the other nations of the world. Instead of amending the Articles of Confederation, the convention developed an entirely new document, guided mainly by James Madison. In September the proposed Constitution of the United States was sent to the state legislatures for approval. In many of the legislatures there was heated debate about giving up states' rights, but by June 1788, a majority of them had finally voted to ratify the new Constitution. The new government established a balance of three powers of government: the Supreme Court, the two houses of Congress, and the newly created executive office of president. George Washington was elected to the position and John Adams was soon to travel back to the United States to assume the office of vice president.

There was one more task for Adams before he departed. He and Jefferson had to meet in Amsterdam to plan negotiations with Dutch bankers to whom the United States owed money. The difficulty of collecting taxes from the individual states had made it almost impossible to pay off the loans. Now the Dutch bankers were threatening to withdraw their financial support. Adams thought the bankers were bluffing but Jefferson did not think so. Finally, just before he departed for America, Adams agreed that Jefferson might persuade them to wait for payment until the new Constitution went into effect. Jefferson's negotiations were successful and he returned to Paris by way of the vineyards of the Rhine Valley. As he traveled through the agricultural countryside, he designed a new type of plow, which he later tested and perfected at Monticello.

As a diplomat, Jefferson had to declare himself neutral in the controversy over the ratification of the Constitution. Privately, he was in favor of strengthening the central government but he thought this could have been achieved by amending the Articles of Confederation. To Madison and others, he expressed some reservations about the new Constitution. In particular, he was deeply concerned that it lacked a bill of rights to guarantee individual citizens' liberties such as the freedom of speech, freedom of religion, the right of assembly, and the right to trial by jury. But on the whole, Jefferson wrote to a few friends, he was pleased with the example of "a government reformed by reason alone without bloodshed."

Reform was developing differently in France. Throughout the summer of 1788 there were riots in Paris. In September martial law was imposed and calm was restored when the king and his ministers agreed to convene the Estates-General in the spring of 1789. The Estates-General, a governmental assembly made up of clergy, nobles, and municipal representatives, had not been called to meet for a hundred and seventy-five years. Jefferson thought that the meeting called for was a good first step in the sharing of government. He believed that the process would be gradual, as his travels outside Paris had shown him that the people of the countryside were so accustomed to tyranny that they were not yet prepared for self-government. Nevertheless, Jefferson concluded that it was time to get his daughters safely home to Virginia. In November 1788, he applied for a six-month leave to take the girls home in April 1789, catch up on neglected business at Monticello, and return to France in the autumn.

The transition of government from the Articles of Confederation to the new Constitution caused a long delay and Jefferson had to remain in Paris for the rest of 1789. As a result, he was present on May 4 to observe the splendor of the first meeting of the Estates-General.

Storming the Bastille, July 14, 1789.

In later meetings there was controversy about the voting regulations and procedures. King Louis XVI began massing foreign mercenary troops at his palace in Versailles near Paris, and in Paris itself mobs began to gather. On July 14, an angry mob stormed the Bastille, an ancient fortress and prison hated by the people as a symbol of the king's tyranny. The commandant was killed and the seven inmates released. Today the date is celebrated as the anniversary of the beginning of the French Revolution.

In August, Jefferson received notice that his leave of absence had been granted, but by then he was much too interested in observing the second revolution of his lifetime to be excited about leaving the country. In fact he had become more than an observer of history-making events. Earlier in the summer, at the request of Lafayette, he had supplied notes and comments on the rights of man so that the marquis might present a declaration to the Estates-General. On August 25, Lafayette urged Jefferson, "for liberty's sake," to host a dinner for eight members of the National Assembly who disagreed with one another about how a new French government might be formed. The next day Jefferson's guests debated the issues for six hours and reached an agreement. As a foreign diplomat, Jefferson had to keep out of the negotiations. The following morning, he went to Versailles to explain to the French foreign minister why matters important only to France had been openly discussed by Frenchmen in the home of a foreigner. Minister the comte de Montmorin seemed already aware of the meeting and even condoned it.

In September, Jefferson prepared to return to the United States and on October 7 he left France with his two daughters and two slaves. William Short remained in Paris to manage the embassy until Jefferson's return in the spring of 1790. When he arrived in Virginia, however, he learned that President Washington had asked him to be secretary of state. Jefferson would have preferred to return to France but it was hard to refuse the president's wishes. The Senate had already confirmed the nomination, there was strong popular support for it, and Madison told him that he must not disappoint the public. While

Jefferson weighed his decision for two months, Patsy was courted by Thomas Mann Randolph Jr., a distant cousin she had known since childhood. In mid-February, Jefferson accepted the appointment but stated in his letter to the president that he could not travel immediately to the temporary capital at New York. Jefferson wanted to wait two weeks to attend his beloved daughter's wedding at Monticello.

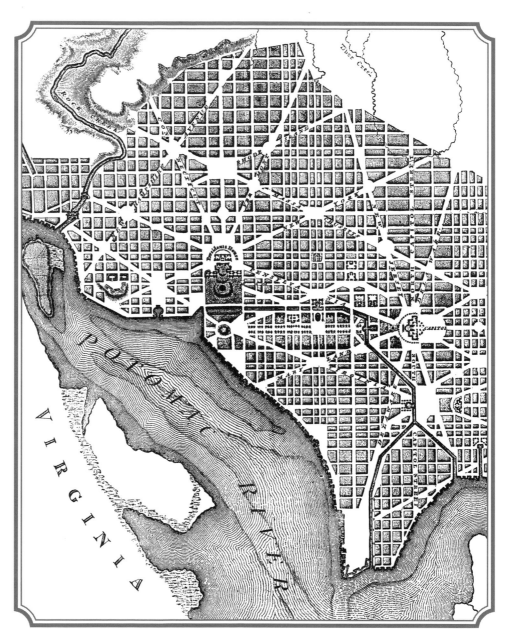

Pierre Charles L'Enfant's plan of Washington, D.C., 1793.

CHAPTER SIX

A New Kind of Government

In 1790 the fresh young United States government began an intense period of inventing traditions. The great variety of tasks all demanded immediate attention. After his first six weeks as Washington's secretary of state, Jefferson was stricken with one of his severe migraine headaches, but even that could not stop his creative mind. During the week or two of recuperation, he drew up a report on international weights and measures based on the decimal system. Congress refused to act on his suggestions and a metric system invented in France eventually became the international standard. One unlikely task of the secretary of state was to sit on a committee of three to set up a national patent system. Jefferson felt that inventors should be encouraged by being permitted temporary exclusive rights to the profits from useful devices they had designed. Abstract ideas, however, cannot be possessed like objects and so Jefferson thought it was natural that "ideas should freely spread . . . for the moral and mutual instruction of man." One may patent a machine that can print an essay on freedom, and even copyright the specific phrasing of the essay, but the U.S. Patent Office cannot grant exclusive rights to the concept of freedom.

Another important matter for the First Congress to consider was the location of a permanent capital for the new nation. At a dinner hosted by Jefferson, an agreement was worked out making Philadelphia the temporary capital for ten years while a brand new "Federal City" was being built on the banks of the Potomac River. Jefferson thought that President Washington should have complete authority over the project, but he intended to assume an active role as advisor. The president picked the site himself and, to supervise the work, selected three commissioners, who later named the city Washington. He relied heavily on his secretary of state to help settle the various squabbles that broke out involving landowners, the commissioners, and Pierre Charles L'Enfant, the French architect in charge of laying out the city. Between 1790 and 1792, Jefferson took a meticulous interest in how each building would look, sometimes offering his own sketches to the architects.

The new Department of State faced its first serious international crisis in May 1790. Near the Pacific Northwest, off Vancouver Island, several British ships were captured by the Spanish. It looked as though there would be war between England and Spain. The British ordered the governor general of Canada, Sir Guy Carleton, first baron Dorchester, to find out what the United States might do if war broke out. Dorchester sent Major George Beckwith on an unofficial mission to gather intelligence on the question. Beckwith began with a person he already knew, Alexander Hamilton, secretary of the treasury.

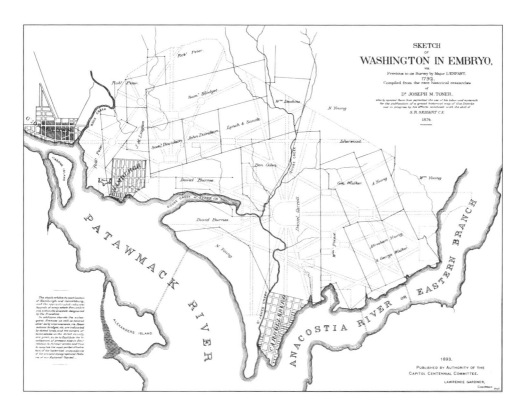

Map showing landowners' properties affected by L'Enfant's plan of Washington.

Pierre Charles L'Enfant.

Hamilton, who had been on Washington's staff during the Revolution, interpreted the inquiry to be a suggestion that the United States should side with Great Britain and reported this to the president. Jefferson was horrified at the idea of an alliance with the former enemy. He was also extremely upset that the secretary of the treasury would dare to usurp the role of the secretary of state by attempting to initiate foreign policy.

This was the beginning of the serious friction between Jefferson and Hamilton that would strain Washington's patience during his first administration. The matter was far more serious than a squabble over ships on the Pacific coast. If England won the war, she would probably take over the Spanish possessions of Louisiana and the Floridas. After the Revolutionary War the British had never withdrawn from their outposts in the area between the Ohio and upper Mississippi Rivers. If they also gained control of the mouth of the Mississippi, navigation of the entire river, serving the commerce of all the lands west of the Appalachian Mountains, would then be under the influence of Great Britain. The people of these American territories might not be interested in forming new states to join the union. By possessing Canada to the north, controlling the Mississippi Valley to the west, and deploying a powerful navy at sea to the east and south, Britain could have the fragile young nation surrounded. To Jefferson, the possibility was a nightmare.

On the other side of the world another controversy arose over the Barbary States on the North African coast of the Mediterranean. The Barbary pirates were continuing to capture ships except for those belonging to countries who paid annual tribute such as England. Jefferson thought it was necessary to raise the money to build a fleet that could eliminate piracy in the Mediterranean. Hamilton felt that to make war on the Barbary States would offend England and he saw to it that his friends in the Senate allowed a proposal for a naval force to die in committee.

Another confrontation between Jefferson and Hamilton began when Hamilton submitted a proposal to Congress for the establishment of a national bank to aid the country in collecting taxes and borrowing money. In Congress, Madison led strong opposition to the bill but it passed. When it was sent to President Washington for his signature, he asked several cabinet members to submit private opinions. Jefferson wrote that the establishment of a bank was not specifically authorized by the Constitution and was therefore a matter to be

Alexander Hamilton, Jefferson's adversary in Washington's cabinet.

decided by the people of the individual states. Aside from regarding the bill as unconstitutional, he thought it would threaten the independence of small farmers throughout the country by putting too much power in the hands of a few wealthy people. Hamilton had no worries over the concentration of wealth and argued that if a procedure or institution was not specifically forbidden by the Constitution it was all right to consider it. The bill became law but the constitutional debate became a recurring theme in the political history of the United States. The constitutional issue of the Civil War was states' rights versus federal authority and in our own time we still argue strict versus loose interpretations of the language of our Constitution.

In addition to creating a permanent national debate, the conflict between Jefferson and Hamilton started the development of political parties. To promote his own agenda, Hamilton wrote anonymous articles attacking Jefferson and his views. Most of these were published under pseudonyms in a newspaper called the *Gazette of the United States.* In response, Jefferson encouraged Madison and other friends to found an opposition paper in Philadelphia called the *National Gazette.* Both Jefferson and Madison believed that the formation of strong political factions would lead to confrontation and divisions among the people throughout the country. They saw the Congress as a forum where discussion and compromise could smooth out factional differences. Nevertheless, they felt it was necessary to publicize and defend their concept of the rights of the common man or see them obliterated by what they regarded as a trend toward monarchy.

In the summer of 1792, the media war between the two newspapers had become so inflammatory that Washington sent separate letters to Jefferson and Hamilton urging them to make peace. Jefferson wrote a long letter of apology and explanation and stated he would retire in March 1793 at the end of Washington's term of office. Hamilton wrote a letter claiming that Jefferson was out to get him and that the bitterness between them was so strong that the president should consider replacing both secretaries. Washington had meant to retire at the end of one term, but Madison urged Washington to run

George Washington,
first President under
the new Constitution.

again for "the interests of your country," and Jefferson wrote to him that if he left office at this point the nation would not survive. Washington ran unopposed in the election of 1792 and was not allied with any faction, but the congressional elections showed an anti-Hamilton tendency. Jefferson analyzed them as "in favor of republican and against aristocratical candidates."

Jefferson had started packing for his return to Monticello, but a month before Washington began his second term in March 1793, he informed the president that he had changed his mind. So that people would not think he was running away from Hamilton's continuing newspaper attacks, he wished to stay in office for another few months. In this year, many heads of the French nobility were sliced off by the guillotine, and then other citizens were executed in the bloody whirlwind of revolution that came to be called the Reign of Terror. Events moved so fast that it was impossible to keep up with them on the western side of the Atlantic. In September 1792, a new National Convention had abolished the monarchy and declared France a republic. In January 1793, King Louis XVI had been guillotined. In February, France had declared war on England. In April, the minister from the Republic of France, Edmond Charles Genêt, arrived in Charleston, South Carolina, and was cheered all the way to Philadelphia.

Meanwhile, news arrived that France had declared war on Spain. Genêt was received cordially by the government but was cautioned that Washington had issued a proclamation of neutrality. The United States would not give military aid to France or to any other European nation. Nevertheless, Genêt began to outfit ships in American ports and recruit American seamen for attacks on Spanish Florida. The secretary of state warned him to stop violating United States neutrality

King Louis XVI of France held captive by French revolutionaries.

but Genêt continued his activities. Eventually the situation became so difficult that Washington's cabinet voted to ask the French government to recall Genêt. Before he was to leave, however, his political party in France fell. If he had gone home, he would have been guillotined. Genêt was permitted to remain in the United States and later he married the daughter of Governor George Clinton of New York.

Edmond Genêt,
minister from the
Republic of France.

The steamy heat of August was unusually oppressive in 1793 and an epidemic of yellow fever broke out in Philadelphia. Many people were extremely ill and five thousand died. Politics began to seem insignificant and the government was moved to a temporary location in Germantown outside Philadelphia until the end of November. In December, Congress convened in Philadelphia. Jefferson had participated in the cabinet's preparation of a report for President Washington to deliver on the complicated events of the previous few months. Now he was determined to retire even though the president wanted him to stay on. Twice before, Washington had persuaded him to continue in office but this time Jefferson had had enough. He wanted "to be liberated from the hated occupations of politics," he said, and to return to "my family, my farm, and my books." He was fifty years old.

At Monticello, Jefferson wrote to John Adams, "I return to farming with an ardor which I scarcely knew in my youth." It was work he loved but it was also urgent. During the decade of his absence, neglectful overseers had let his lands become unproductive. Furthermore, Jefferson was seriously in debt. Some of this was inherited, part from his mother's estate and part through his wife from his father-in-law's estate. His salaries in public life were not large and sometimes he had spent his own money on public business. Jefferson had to start making money.

To renew the soil of his fields, Jefferson set up a system of planting crops of wheat, peas, potatoes, corn, and clover in yearly rotation. Most of the crops were needed to feed the people and livestock living on his plantations, but the wheat was intended to be sold for profit. Jefferson had decided to try wheat as his cash crop because it neither depleted the soil nor required as much slave labor as tobacco. Also, unlike tobacco, wheat was made into healthful food. For spring planting, Jefferson began experimenting with the new type of plow he had first sketched while traveling in France. To reduce the need for slave labor at harvest time he built a mechanical threshing machine that was powered by horses and could be moved from field to field. Despite these imaginative efforts, the wheat crops did not generate enough money for Jefferson's needs. To add to his income he started a nail factory at Monticello. Jefferson was aware that running a business contradicted his philosophy of the agrarian life but he could not make enough money at farming until his lands were productive again. The slaves at the factory were learning a good trade and some of them were even paid small wages as an incentive to work. The factory showed a profit but it did not make as much money as planned because it was difficult to market the nails.

The limited income might have been enough to maintain Monticello as it stood, but influenced by the newer mansions he had seen in France, Jefferson decided to double its original size. His concept was to make a spacious house that appeared to be one story with soaring ceilings in the public areas but had some private upper-story rooms reached by hidden stairways. The main structure was to be topped with a dome based on the one on the Halle aux Bleds in Paris. To begin the expensive project, much of the original building had to be torn apart, and for the next few years, living at Monticello was rather like camping in a lumberyard.

With nearly all of his time and energy devoted to problems of agriculture and architecture, Jefferson stayed out of public affairs. Privately, however, he continued to comment on events in letters to James Madison. In 1794, Washington led a military force of fourteen thousand to western Pennsylvania to put down the Whiskey Rebellion, a series of violent demonstrations by farmers protesting a tax on the whiskey they distilled for market. Jefferson sympathized with farmers struggling to make a living and wrote to Madison that he had heard the militia was laughed at by the local people along the march. The objection to one small tax would now grow into general "detestation of the government." The operation had been a gross overreaction on the part of the federal government. On another issue, Jefferson commented that a controversial treaty with Great Britain, negotiated by John Jay, was an "alliance . . . against the legislature and people of the United States." As Jay was strongly supported by

Hamilton and the Federalists in Congress, Jefferson regarded the treaty as "the boldest act . . . to undermine the constitution" through partisan politics.

The Republicans in Congress wanted Jefferson to run for president in the election of 1796, but he urged Madison to run. "The little spice of ambition which I had in my younger days," he wrote, "has long since evaporated." Nevertheless, when Washington announced his retirement, Jefferson was put forward as the Republican candidate with New Yorker Aaron Burr for vice president. They ran against the Federalist ticket of John Adams and Thomas Pinckney of South Carolina. It was the first two-party election in U.S. history but the parties were not identical to our modern ones. In their sympathy for the common peo-

Left: Aaron Burr. Right: Thomas Pinckney.

ple, Jefferson's Republicans were somewhat like twentieth-century Democrats. In their approach to financial issues, the Federalists resembled modern Republicans. Both candidates chose to stay at home and neither one participated personally in the campaign, but otherwise it was just as mean as twentieth-century elections. The Federalists claimed that Jefferson's pro-French party wanted to overthrow the government and the Republicans called Adams "an avowed monarchist."

In 1796 there was no popular voting for national office. Each state decided how it would select its presidential electors and when these representatives were to vote on the candidates. The balloting began in the late autumn, but because each state voted at a different time and information was transmitted by riders on horseback, the final count was not known until mid-January 1797. The election laws established in 1787 did not anticipate the rise of political parties and simply specified that the candidates were all in the running together. The one who received the most electoral votes became president and the second became vice president. Adams won with seventy-one electoral votes and Jefferson trailed by only three votes, making him the new vice president. Pinckney got fifty-nine votes and Burr only thirty. Some people wondered if Jefferson would accept second place in a Federalist government, but he wrote to Madison that, as Adams was "the only sure barrier against Hamilton's getting in," he was willing to work with his old friend and colleague.

On his way to the inauguration, Jefferson intended to slip into Philadelphia anonymously, riding in a public coach from Alexandria, Virginia. Some of his supporters found out, however, and he was greeted with a booming artillery salute and a banner above the road

John Adams, second
president of the
United States.

Thomas Jefferson,
vice president.

that read "Jefferson the Friend of the People." As soon as he arrived, Jefferson went to pay his respects to president-elect Adams and learned that relations with France were growing tense. Adams was planning to send a team of diplomats to France and thought of including Jefferson in the mission, but Jefferson felt that it was not an appropriate role for a vice president. The inauguration on March 4, 1797, was cheerfully nonpartisan. The spirit did not last long, however, because Adams had kept on most of the Hamiltonian members of Washington's cabinet.

The evening before the inauguration, Jefferson was installed as president of the most important scientific organization in the country, the American Philosophical Society, founded by Benjamin Franklin. This nonpolitical event, having nothing to do with the inauguration, must have pleased Jefferson immensely. A week or so later, the society heard its secretary read Jefferson's paper on the fossil remains of a prehistoric animal, discovered in western Virginia, that was three times the size of a modern lion. Jefferson may have been embarrassed to hear his own comment on the size of the creature read aloud. Nature, he had written, may have "formed the larger animals of America, like its lakes, its rivers, and its mountains on a greater and prouder scale than the other hemisphere." Fortunately, in subsequent papers Jefferson avoided such unscientific boasts, and today paleontologists regard him as an important pioneer in their field.

Less satisfying than activities at the American Philosophical Society was a controversy being debated in the newspapers when Jefferson arrived in Philadelphia. A year before, in a private letter to an Italian friend, Jefferson had written some bluntly partisan remarks about politics in the United States, commenting that "an Anglican monarchical, and aristocratical party" intended to impose a British style of government on the American people. No names were mentioned but the "aristocratical party" had to mean the Federalists. The letter was translated into Italian and published by a newspaper in Florence, Italy. Then the Italian version was translated into French and published in Paris. The Parisian version was translated back into English and published in New York. Even without the additions and misinterpretations made by the various translators, the contents of Jefferson's letter would have made trouble. Jefferson decided not to comment on the controversy for fear of adding to the conflict between the two parties.

Nevertheless, he increased the tension when he joined Aaron Burr and Albert Gallatin, the new Republican leader in Congress, aboard the ship that brought home the returning minister to France, James Monroe. The meeting looked very much like a conference of party

James Monroe, Jefferson's student and colleague.

leaders. Conflict between Federalists and Republicans escalated again in the spring of 1798 with the unfolding of what came to be known as the XYZ Affair. In Paris, the French foreign minister had refused to meet with a commission of American diplomats sent to discuss several grievances, including the capture of American ships by French privateers. Jefferson felt the French hostility was inspired by a statement Adams had made to Congress saying the French were treating the Americans "neither as allies or friends, nor as a sovereign state." In the copy of diplomatic reports sent to Congress, X, Y, and Z were the code names of the French representatives with whom the American mission had hoped to confer.

Anticipating war with France, Secretary of State Timothy Pickering sent pamphlets containing the XYZ material throughout the country, while the Federalists in Congress established a navy department and a standing army. Believing France had no desire for war, Jefferson urged Americans everywhere to cool down. "A little patience, and we shall see the reign of witches pass over," he wrote, "and the people . . . restoring their government to its true principles."

The war fever sweeping the country gave strength to the Federalists, and Congress, remembering the difficulties with Edmond Genêt, passed the first Alien Act on June 25, 1798. This temporary peacetime law gave President Adams the power to deport any alien he considered dangerous to the United States. Jefferson saw it as a political effort to get rid of foreigners who supported the Republicans. He had little objection to a second and permanent Alien Act that was passed on July 6 for the imprisonment or deportation of enemy aliens in time of war. On July 14, however, Congress passed the Sedition Act making it illegal, in both war and peace, for citizens to oppose the government or its officers by insurrection, by writing, or even by speaking.

To Jefferson, the new alien and sedition laws were blatantly unconstitutional. He believed that only the various states, not the federal government, had the right to outline new powers not specifically named in the Constitution. Furthermore, the Sedition Act seemed a clear violation of the right of assembly and the freedom of speech. States' rights and civil liberties were in serious jeopardy. By October 1798, Jefferson had drafted a document that would form the basic language of resolutions objecting to the new laws to be presented in the legislatures of Virginia and the new state of Kentucky. The authorship of the original document was kept secret, because if it became public knowledge that the vice president was involved in political opposition to the government, he could have been accused of sedition. Refined by other authors, the Virginia and Kentucky Resolutions established the principles of states' rights that are still debated in Congress today. They were also the opening issues of the presidential campaign of 1800. In the election of 1796, Jefferson had been a reluctant candidate, remarking that he had "no ambition to rule over men." Now that the Constitution and perhaps even the survival of the republic seemed in grave danger, he took an active role in planning his campaign for the presidency.

In 1800, most of the United States population of roughly five million lived along the eastern seaboard. Transportation by sea, always subject to wind, weather, and tide, was often impossible in winter months. Land communications were also rough and irregular. Three times a week, a stagecoach carried the mail at four miles an hour on a bumpy three-day journey between Boston and New York. From New York to

Philadelphia was a two-day coach ride, and the road on to Baltimore was only sometimes in fair condition. The trail to Washington, D.C., where the government had moved that summer, was a dirt track through the woods that was dangerously muddy during rainy seasons. In the southern states there were practically no stagecoach routes and the mail was carried on horseback. Candidates for national political office did not travel around the country making speeches. Newspapers and pamphlets were the primary means of distributing political information.

"The engine is the press," explained Jefferson in a letter to Madison about campaign strategy. To avoid charges of sedition, he defined the issues and stated Republican principles in secret letters to friends and writers who then passed the information along to the newspapers. The letters were composed during the summer of 1800 at Monticello along with another of Jefferson's projects, a manual of parliamentary rules for the Senate that is still used today in Congress and in state legislatures. He also contributed money to help some of the Republican editors and writers who had tangled with the Sedition Act. One, a man named James Thompson Callender, who had fled Great Britain to avoid prosecution for his writings, had been sentenced to nine months in prison for publishing scandalous stories about President Adams. Although he had encouraged Callender's slanderous work, Jefferson himself refrained from making personal comments about Adams and concentrated on attacking Federalist policies. Most of his supporters followed the example, but a few wanted to generate excitement. *Aurora,* the leading Republican paper, owned by Ben Franklin's grandson, Benjamin Franklin Bache, stated bluntly, "The friends of peace will vote for Jefferson—the friends of war will vote for Adams. . . ."

The Federalists fought back. In a sermon reprinted in many news-papers, the Reverend Timothy Dwight, president of Yale, ranted that if Jefferson was elected, it would be the end of "those morals which protect our lives from the knife of the assassin, which guard the chastity of our wives and daughters from seduction, defend our property from plunder and devastation and shield our religion from contempt and profanation." The *Connecticut Courant,* a Hartford newspaper, predicted that if Jefferson got elected, "murder, robbery, rape, adultery and incest will all be openly taught and practiced." The presidential campaign of 1800 became as dirty as any we have known in our own time.

The Reverend Timothy Dwight, president of Yale in 1800, regarded presidential candidate Jefferson as immoral.

The election was a tie. After three months of balloting throughout the states, Jefferson and Burr each received seventy-three electoral votes, Adams sixty-five, Pinckney sixty-four, and John Jay one. According to the Constitution an electoral tie would have to be settled in the House of Representatives with each state allowed one vote. With the additions of Vermont in 1791, Kentucky in 1793, and Tennessee in 1796, there were now sixteen states. In order to be elected, a candidate was required to win nine of them. The first ballot on February 11 gave eight votes to Jefferson, six to Burr, with two states divided. Thirty-four more ballots were taken during the next seven

The White House, then called the President's House, as it looked when Jefferson was elected.

days with the same results. Hamilton, who hated both men, had been writing to colleagues for weeks. In one letter he wrote, "Jefferson is to be preferred. He is by far not so dangerous a man and he has pretensions to character." The behind-the-scenes campaign finally tipped the balance. On February 17, the thirty-sixth ballot gave Jefferson ten votes.

The Federalist Party of Washington and Adams was defeated. The Republicans had established the two-party system and the people of the young country had achieved a transfer of power without violence or bloodshed. Later, Jefferson called it "the revolution of 1800."

President Jefferson.

CHAPTER SEVEN

President Jefferson

It was the first year of the nineteenth century and Washington, D.C., was still under construction. On March 4, 1801, when he stepped out the door of an ordinary boardinghouse and into the unpaved streets of the new capital, President-elect Thomas Jefferson was dressed in a plain dark suit. Unlike his two predecessors, he was not wearing a ceremonial sword and he did not climb into an elegant carriage to ride in splendor to his inauguration. Accompanied by a group of congressmen and escorted by some officers of the Alexandria militia, the fifty-seven-year-old philosopher of Monticello walked up Jenkins Hill, now called Capitol Hill, to the construction site of the Capitol building. The west wing was the only completed part of the structure and the oath of office was to be administered there in the Senate Chamber.

In his quietly spoken words of the first inaugural address given in Washington, Jefferson made it clear that he intended to establish a

The west wing was the only completed part of the United States Capitol when Jefferson became president.

fresh cooperative spirit in the country. "Though the will of the majority is in all cases to prevail . . . the minority possess their equal rights, which equal law must protect," he reminded his audience. "But every difference of opinion is not a difference of principle. We are all republicans, we are all federalists," he continued. "Sometimes it is said that man cannot be trusted to govern himself. Can he, then, be trusted with the government of others? . . . Let history answer this question." Jefferson then pointed out that the isolation of a spacious continent, protected from the "exterminating havoc" of the Old World by a "wide ocean," was an ideal setting for this experiment in self-government. Its principles would include, "peace, commerce, and honest friendship with all nations . . . the support of State governments . . . the preservation of the General government in its whole constitutional vigor . . . freedom of religion, freedom of the press, and freedom of person under the protection of . . . trial by juries." In closing, he asked for a blessing: "And may that Infinite Power which rules the destinies of the universe lead our councils to what is best."

Jefferson's clear statements announced a new government but the principles mentioned were main timbers in the architecture of his thought even before he wrote the Declaration of Independence. His faith in self-government stemmed from his study of the Enlightenment philosophers and the concept of the natural goodness of people in a state of nature. The unexplored continent of North America was the state of nature he had in mind. His references to the protection of minority opinion and to "freedom of the press" demonstrated his opposition to the Sedition Act. In a delayed response to Federalist charges of atheism, Jefferson spent some evenings in 1804 extracting the words of Jesus from the Gospels for a project he eventually called *The Life and Morals of Jesus,* now known as *The Jefferson Bible.* But the original hurt he felt during the election may have inspired his reference to an "Infinite Power" in the closing words of his inaugural address.

In a last-minute move to hang on to power, a number of new Federalist judges had been appointed by John Adams during the final hours of his presidency and hastily confirmed by the old Senate. One of these appointees was Chief Justice of the Supreme Court John Marshall, who now came forward after the inaugural address to

*Chief Justice
John Marshall.*

administer the oath of office to Jefferson. The two tall Virginia lawyers were cousins, yet they would become bitter political opponents throughout the next eight years. Another last-minute appointee was a justice of the peace for the District of Columbia named William Marbury. His commission did not reach him before the inauguration, and Jefferson, annoyed at the Federalists' desperate efforts, instructed Secretary Madison to withhold it. Marbury sued. Two years later, Chief Justice Marshall would rule in Marbury's favor. An additional part of the opinion written by the chief justice in the case of *Marbury v. Madison* set the legal precedent for judicial review, the right of the Supreme Court to decide if a law passed by the Congress is acceptable according to the Constitution.

In his own government appointments, Jefferson originally intended to stick to the spirit of his inaugural address and did not set out to fire every Federalist left. "No man who has conducted himself according to his duties," he wrote, "would have anything to fear from me . . . be their political principles what they might." On the other hand, he added that since the Federalists had been "in exclusive possession of all offices since the very first origin of party . . . it is now perfectly just that the Republicans should come in for the vacancies which may fall." Eventually, Jefferson did not wait for vacancies and found other ways of replacing Federalists with Republicans in order to establish a fairly even balance between the two parties. For his cabinet appointments, however, he chose a loyal group who would support a new style of leadership, intended to avoid windy debates and time-wasting confrontations. The strongest positions were reserved for two men of brilliance, Swiss-born Albert Gallatin as secretary of the treasury and James Madison as secretary of state. Joining with these two lieutenants,

Secretary of State James Madison and Secretary of the Treasury Albert Gallatin.

Jefferson formed a triumvirate that would become the main strength of his presidency. Throughout his years in office, he would call few meetings of his cabinet, depending on the written opinions of its members to help develop executive policy.

Writing was the main means of communication for the Jefferson administration. A typical day at the President's House, as the White House was then called, began at five in the morning when Jefferson, clad in comfortable old clothes and slippers, sat at his desk to write letters and messages until nine. Then, still wearing the same clothes, he would stop for a while to meet visiting cabinet officers and members of Congress. His day ended with more writing from evening until bedtime at ten. The only exercise he got was an hour or two in the middle of the day when he went horseback riding in the woods around Washington. The only public appearances he made were to host his elegant but relaxed small dinners held three afternoons a week and often arranged by Madison's charming wife, Dolley. The dozen or so guests were served French cuisine along with excellent French wines. Political discussions were not permitted at the table. Jefferson intended that, in a social setting with wives present, genial relationships should form among politicians, foreign diplomats, and members of the cabinet.

The new president and his cabinet had to be the engine of government until the next Congress convened in December 1801. Jefferson's first executive act was to pardon James Thompson Callender and another writer imprisoned under the Sedition Act and call off the legal proceedings in Philadelphia against the editor of the Republican newspaper *Aurora*. Callender then demanded a reward for his work for the Republicans. He asked Jefferson to fire the Richmond postmaster, who happened to be a Federalist, and give the job to Callender. When Jefferson refused, Callender hinted that he had information he would use to hurt the president.

The first international crisis faced by the cabinet was the old problem of the Barbary pirates attacking American ships in the Mediterranean. Reacting to reports from Tripoli, Jefferson had ordered a squadron of naval cruisers to be formed at Norfolk, Virginia, ready to sail for the Mediterranean to protect American commerce. On May 15, 1801, he called a meeting of the cabinet to discuss whether or not the president had the power to send the squadron in the first place. A

A warship battling Barbary pirates.

more important question was, could the president, without congressional approval, authorize the squadron to fight to destroy the enemy if confrontation led to actual war? The majority of the cabinet felt that, as commander in chief, Jefferson did have the necessary authority. The squadron was sent out, sea skirmishes took place, and Tripoli was blockaded, but the action became a conflict that dragged on until 1804.

In 1804, Lieutenant Stephen Decatur became a U.S. Navy hero when he and his men sneaked into Tripoli Harbor to destroy the captured U.S. frigate Philadelphia.

When Congress convened in December, Jefferson's written opening message made a reference to actions in the Mediterranean, but he
could not yet discuss a situation that would have a dramatic effect on
the growth of the new nation. He had recently learned of a secret
agreement made in 1800: Spain, weakened by European wars, was to
return the territory of Louisiana to France, now ruled by Napoleon
Bonaparte, who was soon to become emperor. The vast area was given
its name by the French explorer Robert Cavelier, sieur de La Salle. In
1682, he had traveled from the Great Lakes down the Mississippi River
to the Gulf of Mexico, claiming all the land drained by the great river
for France and calling it Louisiana in honor of King Louis XIV. The
Seven Years War for European control of North America went badly
for France, and in 1752 she ceded the city of New Orleans and all the
territory west of the Mississippi to Spain. The east side of the river
became United States territory after the American Revolution. On
both sides of the river land transportation was extremely difficult,
especially for freight. Water was the best way to move products to market, and the port through which the commerce of the entire
Mississippi basin had to pass on its way to foreign destinations was
New Orleans.

In February 1802, scandal burst upon the nation. James Thompson
Callender joined the staff of a Federalist newspaper, the Richmond
Recorder, and began writing lurid stories about Jefferson's private life.
In one article he stated that in 1768 Jefferson had attempted to seduce
Betsey Walker, the wife of a good friend and neighbor, John Walker.
Another story claimed that Jefferson maintained a "Congo harem" at
Monticello, presided over by his mistress, the "African Venus," Sally
Hemings. This was the same slave who, at fourteen, had sailed to

England with young Polly Jefferson and then traveled with her to Paris in 1786. Callender wrote that she "went to France in the same vessel with Mr. Jefferson and his two daughters." Federalist papers throughout the country used Callender's articles as the source material for a flood of salacious stories. In public, Jefferson made no comment, but privately, in a letter to Secretary of the Navy Robert Smith, he commented on the story about Mrs. Walker. "I plead guilty to one of their charges, that when young and single I offered love to a handsome lady. I acknowledge its incorrectness. It is the only one founded on truth among all their allegations against me."

Meanwhile, Jefferson's concerned attention was still drawn to the secret negotiations between Spain and France. He did not want New Orleans to fall into the hands of Napoleon, not only because France was once more an international power but because she was headed for a war with England. If England won the war and took New Orleans, one of Jefferson's worst nightmares would become reality. In a letter to the American minister in Paris, Robert R. Livingston, Jefferson wrote, "There is on the globe one single spot, the possessor of which is our natural and habitual enemy. It is New Orleans. The day that France takes possession of New Orleans . . . we must marry ourselves to the British fleet and nation." This was a surprising statement from a man who hated England and was sometimes accused of loving France more than his own country.

Some Federalists, angry that the Spanish governor of the port had violated a treaty by forbidding American merchants to store goods awaiting shipment abroad, urged that the United States simply help themselves to New Orleans by force. Taking New Orleans from Spain might have been easy enough, but by the time an expedition of mili-

Robert Livingston was the U.S. minister to France at the time of the Louisiana Purchase.

tias went down the Mississippi to do the job, the enemy might be France, not Spain. Jefferson, aware that France and England would almost certainly go to war, saw no reason to get caught up in a dangerous international conflict. Perhaps the United States could persuade France to sell New Orleans. He instructed Livingston to start negotiations with French foreign minister Charles Maurice de Talleyrand-Périgord. Congress authorized an expenditure of $2 million for the purchase and sent Jefferson's trusted protégé James Monroe to help negotiate. For weeks, while Monroe was at sea, Livingston got nowhere with the French government. Suddenly, on April 11, 1803, Talleyrand asked what the United States would pay for the whole

The port of New Orleans about 1800.

Louisiana Territory. Napoleon had given up the idea of a French empire in the New World after his troops failed to put down a slave rebellion in Santo Domingo, now Haiti. He had hoped to make this his headquarters in the Caribbean. It now appeared that defending New Orleans and Louisiana in a major war with England would be difficult if not impossible. Furthermore, Napoleon desperately needed money to finance his European wars. The next day Monroe arrived at the negotiations and by April 29 the two Americans had arranged to pay $15 million for the Louisiana Territory, an area of more than 800,000 square miles, although the specific boundaries were not mentioned in the treaty drawn up April 30, 1803.

Charles Maurice
de Talleyrand-Périgord,
foreign minister
of France under
Napoleon.

Napoleon
Bonaparte.

As summer approached, Jefferson, who usually insisted on spending the hottest months at Monticello, was still sweating in the sticky tidewater humidity of Washington, waiting for word from France. When the astonishing report arrived, he became concerned that he did not have the specific power to acquire territory, but he was willing to compromise his strict interpretation of the Constitution for two reasons. First, he was afraid that Napoleon might change his mind, and second, news of the purchase was winning overwhelming public approval. On October 21, 1803, after hearing the president's message to "forget metaphysical subtleties" temporarily, Congress ratified a treaty that more than doubled the size of the United States. This area, stretching from the Mississippi to the Rocky Mountains, would eventually become the states of Louisiana, Arkansas, Oklahoma, Missouri, Kansas, Nebraska, Iowa, Minnesota, South Dakota, North Dakota, Wyoming, and Montana. Neither France nor the United States had consulted any of the many Indian tribes that inhabited the vast piece of real estate.

Even before sending Monroe to Paris, Jefferson had begun working on a new version of a project that had fascinated him for a long time, the exploration of the land beyond the Mississippi River. Just after the Revolution he had suggested an expedition to counter the effect of a British effort to explore "the country from the Mississippi to California." In 1786, as minister to France, and concerned about possible French plans to colonize the Pacific Coast, he had encouraged John Ledyard in his unsuccessful expedition to travel eastward from the Pacific to the Mississippi. In 1793, while he was secretary of state, he had organized members of the American Philosophical Society to finance a western expedition that had to be stopped in Kentucky

The Louisiana Purchase, 1803, doubled the area of the United States.

when the leader turned out to be a secret French agent. In 1802, Jefferson learned of Alexander Mackenzie's successful trek to the Pacific coast through the Canadian wilderness. In addition to the efforts of France and Great Britain, Russia had set up fur-trading posts on the coast of Alaska. Jefferson felt this three-way European scramble for empire was a serious threat to the interests of the twenty-six-year-old United States.

A book describing Mackenzie's arduous journey inspired Jefferson to feverish activity. He and his personal secretary, Meriwether Lewis, an experienced woodsman, began intense planning. In January 1803, Congress appropriated money for an expedition up the Missouri to establish contact with the Indian tribes living there. Lewis started a crash course in scientific education, including mapmaking, botany, and zoology as well as medical advice from Jefferson's friend Dr. Benjamin Rush of Philadelphia. Supplies were purchased and an expedition coleader enlisted, William Clark of Kentucky. Preparations were so complicated and delayed that the expedition could not leave Pittsburgh to travel down the Ohio River until September 1803. They did not reach the Mississippi until November and therefore had to make winter camp near St. Louis, but in the spring of 1804 the expedition was traveling slowly up the Missouri River.

In early 1804, the major question in Washington was whether or not Jefferson would run for a second term. On February 25, the Republican members of Congress held a caucus in Philadelphia and nominated Jefferson as their candidate. Vice President Aaron Burr, who had come to be widely distrusted, was discarded in favor of Governor George Clinton of New York. Both nominees accepted. "I sincerely regret that the unbounded calumnies of the Federal party have obliged me to throw myself on the verdict of my country," Jefferson announced, "my great desire having been to retire, at the end of the present term, to a life of tranquility." In claiming that the Federalists forced his decision, Jefferson made the opening blast of the campaign. The Federalists revived the Callender stories and accused the Republicans of plotting to destroy the Constitution. To preserve it, conservative northern Federalists even proposed that New England, along with New York and New Jersey, secede from the union. The

Left: Meriwether Lewis. Below: William Clark.

Republican Party was also breaking into factions and some people now called it the Democratic-Republican Party.

Death overshadowed the campaign. Samuel Adams had died in 1803, and in July 1804 another United States founder came to a more violent end. On the New Jersey Palisades, overlooking the Hudson River, Alexander Hamilton was shot in a duel. His killer was Aaron Burr, who was enraged by insults Hamilton had uttered during Burr's unsuccessful campaign for governor of New York. For Jefferson, however, the saddest death was much closer to home. In March, Polly, who had married in 1797, gave birth to a daughter after a difficult preg-

Burr shoots Hamilton.

The woman in this portrait is said to be Polly Jefferson.

nancy. When Jefferson arrived at Monticello on April 4, he found his younger daughter extremely ill. She died two weeks later. On the return trip to Washington, Jefferson kept his mind off his grief by redesigning a mechanical device he had received from the curator of the American Philosophical Society, painter Charles Willson Peale. The polygraph, as the artist called his invention, made copies of letters while the original letters were being written. Jefferson might have experimented with his "portable secretary" when he wrote a mournful letter to his boyhood friend John Page, now governor of Virginia: "The hope with which I had looked forward to . . . resigning public cares . . . is fearfully blighted."

Although Jefferson's personal life seemed dismal, the general prosperity of the times and the great popularity of the Louisiana Purchase helped him win the greatest election victory of the century. He did better than anyone expected, sweeping fourteen out of the sixteen states, including Massachusetts, the stronghold of conservative Federalism. The overwhelming landslide temporarily exhausted the national interest in political events, and the inauguration on March 5, 1805, was a drab anticlimax. A small and quiet crowd in the Senate Chamber strained to hear the president, dressed entirely in black, as he delivered his address. An important part of the speech was about the Indian tribes in danger of being obliterated by white settlers moving into the Mississippi Valley. Indians, Jefferson said, were "endowed . . . with the rights of men." It was therefore important "to teach them agriculture and the domestic arts . . . which alone can enable them to maintain their place in existence." His humanitarian proposal overlooked a sad and difficult question: Must the survival of the Indians cost them their traditional way of life?

International affairs soon drew Jefferson's attention away from the domestic scene. On October 21, 1805, at the Battle of Trafalgar, off the coast of Gibraltar, Admiral Horatio Nelson defeated the French and Spanish fleets, ending Napoleon's naval power and making England ruler of the seas. On December 2, at the Battle of Austerlitz, in what is now the Czech Republic, Napoleon defeated the combined armies of Czar Alexander I of Russia and Emperor Francis II of Austria, making him ruler of the European continent. "What an awful spectacle," commented Jefferson when the news reached Washington in January 1806. "One man bestriding the continent of Europe like a Colossus and another roaming unbridled on the ocean." To reduce European influence in America, Jefferson had worked on plans to buy East and West Florida from Spain, but that hope began to fade with the victory at Austerlitz because Napoleon no longer had an urgent need for money. The disappointment soon became minor compared to another result of the new balance of power in Europe. England began flexing her new sea power in efforts to dominate American commerce.

Admiral Horatio Nelson at the Battle of Trafalgar. In earlier battles he lost an eye and his right arm. At Trafalgar he was killed but the victory made England ruler of the seas.

Emperor Napoleon at the Battle of Austerlitz. The emperor's army defeated two other armies making him the ruler of the European continent.

With his attention sharply focused on affairs in Europe, Jefferson ignored anonymous warnings that former Vice President Aaron Burr was involved in a mysterious scheme to create a new republic in Louisiana. After shooting Hamilton, Burr fled New York and New Jersey where he was wanted for murder and eventually met up with General James Wilkinson, governor of the upper Louisiana Territory. Wilkinson was popularly regarded as a Revolutionary hero but since 1786 he had been secretly accepting money from Spain to form a new nation in the lower Mississippi Valley. In February 1806, Jefferson received a private letter telling him that certain territorial officials were plotting "a separation of the union in favour of Spain." While Jefferson was discussing the problem with his cabinet, Wilkinson, alarmed that rumors of the plot were spreading, turned on his coconspirator. He sent dispatches to Washington in November 1806 accusing Burr of a fantastic plan to seize New Orleans and move on to Mexico with ten thousand men. Jefferson issued a proclamation warning of the conspiracy, unaware that Burr, on his way down the river to Natchez with sixty armed men, had already learned of Wilkinson's treachery and surrendered in the Mississippi Territory.

On December 2, 1806, in his annual message to Congress, Jefferson included a paragraph on the return of Lewis and Clark from their eight-thousand-mile round trip to the Pacific. He did not go into

Lewis and Clark with Sacajawea, the Indian woman who led them across the Rockies, as imagined by the painter of the American West Frederic Remington.

the scientific details, such as the discovery of 178 plant species and 122 animals never before seen by people of European descent. Nor did he mention that the hoped-for water route to the Pacific was blocked by the Rocky Mountains. He did, however, write that trade might be developed with "numerous tribes of Indians hitherto unknown." The arduous journey was a huge success in terms of heroic exploration and scientific knowledge, but the environmental future of the continent was now open to wholesale exploitation. Historian Frederick Jackson Turner, in an essay published in 1893 called *The Significance of the Frontier,* described the slow sweep of human waves that flowed steadily through the Appalachian Mountains during Jefferson's lifetime. "Stand at Cumberland Gap," he wrote, "and watch the procession of civilization . . . the Indian, the fur trader and hunter, the cattle-raiser, the farmer. . . . Stand at South Pass in the Rockies a century later," Turner continued, "and see the same procession." Jefferson had hoped to reserve the land west of the Mississippi for the Indians, but even he could not have stopped the flood of traders and settlers.

The role of slavery in this epic story of national growth was not yet the burning controversy it would become, but in March 1807, Jefferson raised the issue. He reminded Congress that twenty years after ratification, the Constitution provided for the authority to abolish the importation of slaves into the United States. On his recommendation, Congress promptly passed a law that would prohibit the importation of slaves from outside the United States as of January 1, 1808. Jefferson believed that stopping the slave trade was a major step toward the total abolition of slavery. But Congress did not make provisions for the navy to seize ships that were illegally carrying slaves. Therefore, Great Britain was the only power capable of stopping the

Africans on a slave ship.

slave trade on the high seas. An Englishman named William Wilberforce, who led a twenty-year campaign in Parliament for the abolition of slavery, asked President Jefferson to agree to let both the American and the British navies stop slavers at sea. Because the British had recently begun to stop American ships and search them for English sailors, Jefferson was adamantly opposed to permitting the British navy to halt American vessels for any reason.

It was inevitable that British maritime policy would soon provoke an international incident. On June 22, the British man-of-war *Leopard* fired on the United States frigate *Chesapeake* off the coast of Virginia. The commander of the *Leopard* had demanded permission to search the *Chesapeake* for British deserters. The American commander refused, and the British then fired three broadsides at close range, inflicting serious casualties and such heavy damage that the *Chesapeake* was forced to surrender. The British boarding party took four sailors off the crippled ship, three of whom were American citizens who had once volunteered for service in the British navy. A wave of anger swept through American seaports after the leaking *Chesapeake* struggled back to Hampton Roads, Virginia, carrying eighteen wounded sailors and three dead. Many people screamed for war but Jefferson thought it wiser to demand an apology and order all British ships to leave American waters. Later, in Monticello for the summer, he began to think that war with England might be inevitable after all.

While Jefferson brooded about conflict with England, Aaron Burr's trial for treason was held in Richmond, Chief Justice John Marshall presiding. Earlier, during preliminary hearings in May, Marshall had issued a subpoena for Jefferson to appear in court with the government papers relating to Burr's conspiracy with Wilkinson. Jefferson sent the papers but refused to travel to Richmond. "The leading feature of our Constitution," Jefferson explained, "is the independence of the Legislature, Executive, and Judiciary. . . . But would the Executive be independent of the Judiciary if he were subjected to the *commands* of the latter, and to imprisonment for disobedience?" In August, Marshall instructed the jury on the rules of evidence in the case. He based them on Article 3, Section 3, of the Constitution, which states, "No person shall be convicted of treason unless on testimony of two witnesses to the same overt act." As Burr had not been present at Blennerhassett's Island, where the sixty armed men first gathered, no one could have witnessed him actually committing the "overt act" of assembling troops to make war on the United States. Even though Jefferson understood Article 3 of the Constitution, he chose to believe that Marshall's ruling was politically motivated. His anger subsided, however, at the thought that the verdict would be so unpopular that it would start a movement for a constitutional amendment regarding treason.

When he returned to Washington in the fall, Jefferson was again hoping for peace with Great Britain until he learned that diplomatic talks in London had broken down. Even worse, King George III issued an order to English naval officers requiring the impressment, or seizure, of seamen, British or American, naval or merchant, to fill out understaffed British navy crews. In December 1807, at Jefferson's urgent request, Congress passed an act to stop all export cargoes from leaving American ports. This embargo was intended to hurt Great Britain by depriving her of American trade, but within the year a dismal economic depression gripped the United States and smugglers were making a mockery of the policy. In the south, goods were transported into Spanish Florida and then abroad. In the north, fine timber, livestock, and surplus crops were shipped through Lake Champlain or the Great Lakes to Canada for eventual transfer to England. Efforts to control these remote trade routes resulted in local rebellions. Secretary of the Treasury Gallatin, who had opposed the embargo from the beginning, stating, "Government prohibitions do always more mischief than had been calculated," now advised Jefferson to mobilize regular troops to quell the insurrections and send navy gunboats to patrol Lake Champlain. Instead of attacking England, the American military forces were making war on the American people.

Although the failing embargo cast a dark shadow over Jefferson's final year in office, there was a strong grassroots movement for him to run again. Refusing to set the precedent for a third term, Jefferson supported his protégé James Madison for president. As early as November 1807, Dolley Madison and her husband had begun hosting

Dolley Madison, wife of James Madison, frequently acted as hostess for President Jefferson's official dinners.

dinner parties to promote his candidacy. Madison won the nomination and the election, doing well throughout the nation except in New England, where the embargo had caused a devastating economic depression. Jefferson's last message to Congress in November 1808 noted that at least the embargo had saved some lives and given the United States time to prepare for war. On March 1, 1809, a weary Jefferson signed the repeal of the embargo. Of his forthcoming retirement he wrote to a friend, "Never did a prisoner released from his chains, feel such relief as I shall on shaking off the shackles of power."

At the inaugural ball on March 3, 1809, the first dance Jefferson had attended since the death of his wife in 1782, some of the guests noted that he seemed much happier than President Madison, who was looking pale and tense. "I have got this burden off my shoulders," said Jefferson, "while he has now got it on his."

Thomas Jefferson at seventy-eight. In painting this portrait, the artist,
Thomas Sully, smoothed the wrinkles of age.

CHAPTER EIGHT

The Academical Village

he journey home in March 1809 must have reminded Jefferson of the one he and his new bride made thirty-seven years earlier. He wrote to Madison that the last three days on horseback had included eight hours of riding "through as dis-agreeable a snow storm as I was ever in." Friends in Albemarle County had wanted to meet him on the road with a detachment of militia and escort him up the mountain to Monticello. Jefferson declined the honor, writing that simply returning to his neighbors would "make me happier than I have been since I left them." He intended to have a busy retirement full of building projects, scholarly reading, and plenty of time for his grandchildren. In addition, he would at last be able to concentrate on his long-cherished dream for the state of Virginia, a system of public education.

As early as 1777, Jefferson had formed a plan for the "general diffusion of knowledge" in Virginia. It called for dividing each county into small districts called hundreds that would provide free education at the primary level. The counties would provide the secondary level, where students would learn Latin, Greek, and basic science and the best students would go on to William and Mary College. Later, Jefferson decided that his old college was unsatisfactory for the purpose because he thought the curriculum too rigid, the location not conveniently central, and the tidewater climate of Williamsburg unhealthy. The program, as he had outlined it in *Notes on the State of Virginia* in 1781, was considered radical at the time. In 1786, when he was the United States minister to France, Jefferson wrote to George Wythe concerning the revision of Virginia's code of laws that was then taking place in the state legislature. He urged Wythe to start "a crusade against ignorance." He had observed that, although Paris was the brilliant center of European culture and learning, the common people were hopelessly sunk in "ignorance, superstition, poverty and oppression of body and mind." Jefferson went on to state that education was essential to self-government. "No other sure foundation can be devised for the preservation of freedom and happiness." The Tidewater aristocrats who dominated the General Assembly did not agree with Jefferson and by the time he retired in 1809 they still had not voted for any form of public education.

Jefferson had to start a patient struggle just to achieve a part of his general plan and there were other distractions. The worst of these was his dismal financial situation. When he returned to Monticello for good he was in debt for $30,000, an enormous sum of money in those days. A large part of it had been inherited from his father-in-law, and Jefferson's modest salaries when in public office had never enabled him to keep up with debt repayment. In retirement, his income was further reduced. Pensions for retired presidents did not exist at that time. Due to years of neglect, the farming and the nailery were not making much money and certainly could not support Jefferson's elegant living habits. When his daughter Martha was making plans to take over the management of his household, she wrote to her father, "I can bear anything but the idea of seeing you harassed in your old age by debts." Nevertheless, growing debts became a dark shadow looming over Monticello in Jefferson's final years.

Martha Jefferson Randolph by Thomas Sully.

Making a living from Monticello had never been easy. The soil on the mountaintop was not as good for farming as the rich valley lands and Jefferson's overseer, Edmund Bacon, described it as "hard to work." Its quality had been further reduced by tobacco cultivation. As early as 1794, Jefferson had decided to establish wheat as his main cash crop, but wheat farming had its own frustrating problems. When droughts, insects, or blights damaged the crops, the mill produced less flour. If the water of the Rivanna River was low in the fall or clogged with ice in the winter, the barrels of flour could not be shipped to market in Richmond. A small trickle of income came from the nailery but it had to shut down during the War of 1812, when the British blockade of Philadelphia cut off the supply of iron from Pennsylvania. In another effort at manufacturing, Jefferson bought spinning and weaving equipment to produce wool and cotton cloth. Manufacturing of any kind might seem a strange project for a man who distrusted commerce and celebrated the virtues of the agricultural life. His main purpose, however, was to make enough fabric to clothe his family and slaves. Any surplus textile was sold but it was not a major source of income.

Like most Virginia plantation owners, Jefferson figured his wealth in terms of property, not money. Therefore, financial debt did not totally overshadow his enjoyment of life. He played games with his younger grandchildren and saw to the education of the older ones. He also helped with the education of young men who came to him from all over the country. They rented rooms in Charlottesville and had free access to Jefferson's library. There were also many other visitors, not all of them invited. Sometimes the peace of Monticello became so disrupted that Jefferson would travel ninety miles to another house, a

A painting of Jefferson supervising a slave at work.

small octagonal masterpiece he had started building in 1806 on his Poplar Forest estate in Bedford County. By 1812, Jefferson was making three trips a year to enjoy the tranquillity of Poplar Forest, taking along one or two of his older grandchildren for company.

Another pleasure of Jefferson's old age was reconnecting his ties with John Adams. Communication between the two colleagues in revolution had ended in 1800 because of Adams's bitterness over his defeat in the election and Jefferson's anger at the "midnight appointments" made by the outgoing Federalist administration. Their mutual friend and fellow signer of the Declaration of Independence, Dr. Benjamin Rush, had been working on a reconciliation for some time. He wrote to Adams, and later to Jefferson, suggesting that the two former presidents might now think about corresponding, but both made excuses. After the two old patriots had made a few more face-saving comments to Rush, Adams took the opportunity of New Year's Day 1812 to write to Jefferson wishing him "many happy New Years." He also mentioned that he was sending a separate package of two pieces of "homespun." Immediately, Jefferson replied with an essay on the economics of home manufacturing, not realizing that Adams was making a little joke. When the package finally arrived at Monticello, it contained two volumes written by Adams's son, John Quincy Adams. Jefferson and Adams continued to correspond for the rest of their lives.

The home of John and Abigail Adams in Quincy, Massachusetts.

Eighteen twelve, the year that Adams chose to wish happiness for Jefferson, was not so happy for the United States. On June 18, Congress declared war on Great Britain. The reasons included the old issues of violation of commercial neutrality and the impressment of American seamen into the British navy. England and France were already at war and the British wanted to stop American vessels from shipping goods to continental Europe. In addition, some people in the western states believed the British were arming Indian tribes and encouraging them to stop settlers from moving west. Wealthy New England merchants thought a war would only disrupt commerce but a group of western radicals in Congress known as the "war hawks" managed to round up enough votes to declare war on Great Britain. The small United States Navy did surprisingly well at first but Great Britain soon reasserted her overwhelming sea power by blockading American ports. Battles were fought on Lake Erie, Lake Champlain, and in western New York, but American forces failed in their plan to capture Canada. In August 1814, the British captured Washington, D.C., and burned the Capitol.

All three thousand volumes in the Library of Congress were lost in the flames. In 1800, President Adams had approved the first appropriation of funds to establish a congressional library. Later, President Jefferson helped define its purposes, appointed the first two librarians of Congress, and often recommended books to be purchased. When he learned of the loss, Jefferson was appalled and called it an act of barbarism. He offered to sell his own library of 6,487 volumes for whatever price Congress cared to name. The collection, covering a huge variety of subjects, was probably the best library in the country. The section on North and South America was especially outstanding.

The British burning Washington during the War of 1812.

Jefferson described it as "the result of my own personal searches in Paris . . . and of persons employed by me in England, Holland, Germany and Spain." A visitor from Boston wrote that Jefferson's volumes on the Americas were "without a question the most valuable in the world." Others had negative opinions about the general collection. One journalist called it "the grand library of Mr. Jefferson . . . with all its finery and philosophical nonsense," and Jefferson's generous offer provoked debate in Congress. Finally, in 1815 it was purchased for $23,950. After the ten wagons full of books rumbled off to Washington, Jefferson wrote to Adams, "I can not live without books." Then he started a new collection.

In June 1815, Jefferson turned the management of Monticello and his other Albemarle County lands over to one of his grandsons, Thomas Jefferson Randolph, known as Jeff, now married and living at Monticello. This gave Jefferson additional time to concentrate on educational planning. The General Assembly had already rejected one of Jefferson's proposals for general public education beginning at the elementary level as far too expensive, but it was interested in establishing a more advanced institution. In January 1816, the legislature passed a bill, which Jefferson had written, chartering a high school called Central College to be planned by a board of visitors appointed by the governor. On Jefferson's recommendation, Governor Wilson Cary Nicholas appointed Jefferson and his two protégés, James Madison and James Monroe, as well as three other men who were advocates of Jefferson's ideas on education.

In May 1817, Jefferson presented an architectural plan to the board of visitors. The board approved the plan, authorized construction, and started a campaign to raise money. In July, Jefferson staked out the "academical village" on a two-hundred-acre site in Charlottesville. Unlike any other institutions then existing in Europe or America, Central College was to be in the form of a large quadrangle. On the east and west there were to be a series of pavilions, one for each academic discipline, with a faculty apartment attached. In between would be dormitory rooms for the students. At the north end of the quadrangle there would be a large structure to function as a central building and library. An architect, Benjamin Henry Latrobe, who had designed public buildings in Washington and Philadelphia, had already suggested a rotunda as a feature of the campus. Jefferson adopted the idea for the library and drew plans for a round building with a domed roof and pillared portico. In October the cornerstone of the first pavilion was laid by President James Monroe. The other members of the board of visitors were also present, including former presidents Jefferson and Madison.

The Rotunda, first suggested by Benjamin Latrobe, was adopted by Jefferson for the library of his academical village.

Knowing that students coming to the college would first need academic preparation, Jefferson submitted to the legislature yet another plan for a system of statewide public education. The bill was again rejected but the legislature established annual funding for a full-fledged university when a location could be chosen. Jefferson was appointed to the commission to choose the site. It met in August 1818 at Rockfish Gap, twenty miles west of Charlottesville, and promptly elected Jefferson as head. Alternative sites at Lexington and Staunton lost out to Jefferson's plan when most of the members understood that a campus was already under construction at Charlottesville. In January 1819, the General Assembly approved, and a letter came from Richmond informing Jefferson, "Your college is made the University of Virginia." At the time, no one expected that women might study at this or any other university and certainly no one dreamed that the student body would one day include African-Americans.

Slavery was one issue on which Jefferson made no public comment after he retired to Monticello. The man who had often proposed plans for the emancipation of slaves seemed to have forgotten that he had once written the words "all men are created equal." Some historians have noted that Jefferson feared a violent slave rebellion like the one that had taken place in Haiti and did not want to be the person who inspired a similar bloodbath in Virginia. Others have suggested that because he was now living permanently in the midst of a slave-owning society, he did not want to irritate his neighbors by speaking out in favor of emancipation. Still others have thought that because life at his beloved Monticello was totally dependent on slaves, he could not afford to free them. One biographer, Alf J. Mapp Jr., has pointed out that because Jefferson was deeply in debt and slaves were part of

Chained slaves in Washington, D.C., the unfinished Capitol in the background.

his property, his creditors could legally prevent him from freeing them.

Jefferson was tired. In his final years he did not have the energy to fight in every battle. He said as much in a reply to a letter from a friend, Edward Coles, who had freed his slaves and settled them on fifty-acre plots in Ohio. "The love of justice and the love of country," Jefferson wrote, "plead equally the cause of these people. . . . The hour of emancipation is advancing, in the march of time." But he went on to say that he was too old to buckle on a young man's sword and armor to fight for African-American freedom: "This enterprise is for the young; for those who can follow it up. . . . It shall have all my prayers & these are the only weapons of an old man."

If Jefferson had started a campaign for emancipation he would have lost it in Virginia. As he had noted in his letter to Coles, most Virginians were brought up to regard blacks "as legitimate subjects of property as their horses and cattle." Slaveholders usually ignored proposals for emancipation, but they were forced to consider the problem in 1819 when Congress was debating the admission of Missouri as a new state in the union. Even though slavery had always existed in the territory, Congressman James Tallmadge Jr. of New York proposed that it be prohibited in the state. To Jefferson the news came "like a fire-bell in the night." He was terrified that this could mean the breakup of the United States into two countries, one permitting slavery and one prohibiting it. In his mind a strong union of all states was the only way the country could be equal to other nations of the world. He believed, however, that the Constitution allowed the people of each state the right to decide on matters within their own borders, just as he had believed that the colonies should have been entitled to the same right without dictation from Parliament. Interference in the internal matters of a state by other states or by the federal government was, therefore, unconstitutional. When Adams heard of Jefferson's views he refrained from writing about them to his old friend. Adams agreed that constitutional authority should not dictate the internal affairs of individual states, but he believed that slavery was not a constitutional matter. It was a moral issue. Slavery was an evil that should be uprooted.

The debate over the admission of Missouri continued from February 1819 to August 1821. Finally, it was settled by a compromise put together by Speaker of the House Henry Clay of Kentucky and Senator Jesse B. Thomas of Illinois. The admission of Maine as a free state and Missouri as a slave state maintained the previous equal balance. The compromise did not, however, settle the question of states' rights versus constitutional authority, which is still debated today, and it only postponed the controversy over slavery, which led to the American Civil War. Jefferson continued to fear that the union of states forged in 1776 was headed for destruction. In a letter to a Massachusetts congressman he wrote, "My only consolation is to be, that I live not to weep over it." As Jefferson's most famous biographer, Dumas Malone, wrote, "All he hoped to do was open the University of Virginia."

In 1824, at the invitation of President Monroe, Jefferson's old friend the marquis de Lafayette made a ceremonial visit to the United States. He arrived in New York on August 15 and was received so triumphantly by the citizens of the various places he traveled through that he did not get to visit his old comrade at Monticello until November 4. This was just as well as Jefferson was seriously ill during October and would have been a poor host. Lafayette's procession to Monticello was escorted by a magnificently uniformed detachment of the Albemarle Lafayette Guards and groups of local citizens. They all formed a circle at the entrance to make a space for Jefferson to shuffle weakly toward Lafayette's carriage. When he saw Lafayette,

Jefferson's tottering pace speeded slightly, and as the two men hugged each other, tears rolled down their cheeks. The next day, Lafayette was the guest of honor at the first formal dinner held at the still unfinished rotunda of the University of Virginia. Many toasts were made to Jefferson and to Lafayette. Jefferson asked the master of ceremonies to read a written acknowledgment aloud, as his recent illness had left him too feeble to do it himself. The two old heroes then returned to Monticello to rest and talk about old times, and several days later Jefferson escorted his guest on a tour of the new academical village.

French army officer Lafayette, a hero of the American Revolution, toured the United States in 1824, stopping at Monticello to visit his old friend Jefferson.

The University of Virginia opened officially on March 7, 1825. It was not a major event because not all the schools were ready. Textbooks had been delayed. The five members of the faculty recruited in Europe had finally arrived after a difficult voyage but two American professors were not yet in residence. The board of visitors had had no success finding a professor of law. One had declined for reasons of poor health, and several other candidates had declined, perhaps because Jefferson was most particular about what sort of legal scholar should hold the position. Dr. Robley Dunglison, who would soon become Jefferson's personal physician, was to head the school of anatomy and medicine, but he could not teach until the anatomy building was built. The most difficult problem, however, was that the fifty or sixty enrolled students were, as Jefferson wrote, "wretchedly prepared." The temporary solution was to relax the academic requirements, but the situation clearly demonstrated Virginia's urgent need for a good system of elementary and secondary education.

The General Assembly was not much help. In 1824, it had voted to give the university $50,000 a year, but in February 1826, it cut off all funds. As soon as he learned of this, Jefferson rode down to Charlottesville to personally stop most of the ongoing construction and devote what funds were still available to completing the rotunda and the anatomy building. The action of the legislature might seem shortsighted and pinchpenny but the Assembly was faced with an economic depression that had begun in 1819 and was getting worse.

The depression also had a bad effect on Jefferson's personal finances. Land now sold for only a quarter of what it had been worth a decade before and it was difficult to find buyers. Jefferson could no longer hope to pay off old debts by selling some of his farmland. In addition, he had cosigned a $20,000 bank loan to his friend Wilson Cary Nicholas, who then went bankrupt, leaving Jefferson responsible for yet another large debt. In desperation, he came up with a scheme to set up a national lottery with all his lands, except for Monticello, as the prize. According to Virginia law, the plan required the approval of the General Assembly. At first they refused, but after much lobbying by Jefferson's friends, they voted in favor of it with the requirement that Monticello must be included. The blow was made softer by an agreement that Jefferson would be allowed to live at Monticello for the rest

Monticello, east portico. The weathervane on the roof is connected to a dial below so wind direction can be read without stepping outside.

of his life and Martha would be permitted to stay for two more years after his death. No lottery tickets had been sold by the time Jefferson died. His debts then totaled about $100,000. It is impossible to calculate exactly how much this would amount to in today's money but it would have to be roughly estimated as several million dollars.

On February 17, in one of his last letters to James Madison, Jefferson outlined the details of his financial woes and then apologized for imposing them on an old friend. More important to him were the fifty-year friendship and shared political views that "have been sources of constant happiness to me. . . . And if I remove beyond the reach of attentions to the university, or beyond . . . life itself, as I soon must, it is a comfort to leave that institution under your care." In March,

James Madison,
Jefferson's loyal friend
for half a century.

Jefferson wrote his will, in which, among other things, he left a gold-headed cane to Madison, his books to the university, and a watch to each of his grandchildren. He also freed five of his slaves who had learned skills they would need to support themselves. "In doing so," writes Alf J. Mapp Jr., "he was relying on the generosity of his creditors not to block this disposal of property." In April, Jefferson was just strong enough to attend a meeting of the board of visitors. In May he made a brief visit to give specific instructions concerning the portico of the rotunda and he returned in early June to sit in a chair and observe the installation of a capital on the top of one of the rotunda's columns.

Jefferson's University of Virginia dominated by the rotunda is the heart of the modern university, which sprawls through the west side of Charlottesville.

On June 24, Jefferson wrote a letter to the citizens of Washington explaining that his poor health prevented him from accepting their invitation to attend the celebration of the fiftieth anniversary of the Declaration of Independence. He hoped the event would be a signal to people all over the world to "burst the chains" of ignorance and oppression "to assume the blessings and security of self-government." On July 2, Jefferson began to slip in and out of consciousness. At about seven o'clock in the evening of July 3, he awoke long enough to ask feebly, "Is it the fourth?" Dr. Dunglison told him that it soon would be. Shortly past noon on the fourth he died. In Massachusetts, on the same afternoon, John Adams died after saying, "Thomas Jefferson survives."

★   ★   ★

In one sense Adams was correct. Jefferson's concept of the natural rights of individuals still survives in a nation that has grown from a simple rural society into an industrialized world power. But if he could return today, Jefferson would be shocked to see states' rights overshadowed by a strong central government that spends trillions of tax dollars on social programs and a colossal military structure. Furthermore, he would find it incredible that we have become a multicultural nation that tries to tolerate all peoples, including the African-Americans he never completely understood.

Jefferson did not live long enough into the nineteenth century to know of the Great Potato Famine that forced hordes of Irish peasants to leave their homes and cross the sea to Boston, New York, and Chicago. He was not alive at the turn of the century to visit Ellis Island and see the throngs of Italians driven from poverty or the crowds of Jewish refugees from the shtetls of Poland and Russia. He could not have imagined Chinatown in San Francisco or Japanese farmers in the valleys of California. And he never would have thought that naturalized United States citizens might be Catholics from Latin America, Buddhists from Southeast Asia, Muslims from Pakistan, and Hindus from India. But he would have insisted that all of these peoples are entitled by nature to certain human rights. These rights, he would have said, must be preserved by self-government. Intelligent self-government, Thomas Jefferson asserted, depends on enlightened education.

An engraved portrait copied from a sketch by Gilbert Stuart. The family thought the image was the best likeness of Thomas Jefferson.

A few of the six thousand volumes Jefferson sold to the Library of Congress.

In Jefferson's Words

Take things always by their smooth handle.

✶

I never considered a difference of opinion in politics, in religion, in philosophy, as cause for withdrawing from a friend.

✶

I have sworn upon the altar of God eternal hostility against every form of tyranny over the mind of man.

✶

A little rebellion now and then is a good thing, and as necessary in the political world as storms in the physical.

✶

When angry count ten before you speak; if very angry, an hundred.

✶

The earth belongs to the living, not to the dead.

As new discoveries are made, new truths disclosed, and manners and opinions change with the change of circumstances, institutions must advance also, and keep pace with the times.

⋆

We seldom repent for having eaten too little.

⋆

Never trouble another for what you can do yourself.

⋆

A wise and frugal government, which shall restrain men from injuring one another, shall leave them otherwise free to regulate their own pursuits of industry and improvement and shall not take from the mouth of labor the bread it has earned.

⋆

Honesty is the first chapter in the Book of Wisdom.

⋆

He who permits himself to tell a lie once, finds it much easier to do it a second and third time, till at length it becomes habitual; he tells lies without attending to it, and truths without the world's believing him.

⋆

Ignorance is preferable to error; and he is less remote from the truth who believes nothing than he who believes what is wrong.

⋆

The God who gave us life gave us liberty at the same time.

⋆

My confidence in my countrymen generally leaves me without much fear for the future.

⋆

Those who labor in the earth are the chosen people of God, if ever he had a chosen people.

The care of human life and happiness, and not their destruction, is the first and only legitimate object of good government.

✯

There is a natural aristocracy among men. The grounds of this are virtue and talents.

✯

If we can prevent the Government from wasting the labors of the people, under the pretense of taking care of them, they must become happy.

✯

With all the imperfections of our present government, it is without comparison the best existing or that ever did exist.

✯

Establish the law for educating the common people.

✯

Enlighten the people generally, and tyranny and oppressions of body and mind will vanish like evil spirits at the dawn of day.

✯

I know of no safe depository of the ultimate powers of the society but the people themselves; and if we think them not enlightened enough to exercise their control with a wholesome discretion, the remedy is not to take it from them, but to inform their discretion.

✯

Whenever the people are well informed, they can be trusted with their own government.

✯

Education is the true corrective of abuses of constitutional power.

Bibliography

Adams, Henry. *The Formative Years: A History of the United States During the Administrations of Jefferson and Madison.* Condensed and edited by Herbert Agar. Boston: Houghton Mifflin, 1947.

_____. *The United States in 1800.* Ithaca, New York: Cornell University Press, 1962.

Ambrose, Stephen E. *Undaunted Courage: Meriwether Lewis, Thomas Jefferson, and the Opening of the American West.* New York: Simon & Schuster, 1996.

Becker, Carl. *The Declaration of Independence.* New York: Random House, Vintage Books, 1942.

Boorstin, Daniel J. *The Lost World of Thomas Jefferson.* Chicago: University of Chicago Press, 1993.

Brodie, Fawn M. *Thomas Jefferson, an Intimate History.* New York: W. W. Norton, 1974.

Cole, John Y. *Jefferson's Legacy, a Brief History of the Library of Congress.* Washington, D.C.: Library of Congress, 1993.

Cunningham, Noble E., Jr. *In Pursuit of Reason: The Life of Thomas Jefferson.* New York: Ballantine Books, 1988.

Dabney, Virginius. *The Jefferson Scandals: A Rebuttal.* Lanham, Maryland: Madison Books, 1991.

Dos Passos, John. *The Head and Heart of Thomas Jefferson.* Garden City, New York: Doubleday & Company, 1954.

Ellis, Joseph J. *American Sphinx: The Character of Thomas Jefferson.* New York: Alfred A. Knopf, 1997.

Hall, Gordon Langley. *Mr. Jefferson's Ladies.* Boston: Beacon Press, 1966.

Hofstadter, Richard, ed. *Great Issues in American History, Volume I.* New York: Random House, Vintage Books, 1958.

Jefferson, Thomas. *Autobiography of Thomas Jefferson.* New York: Capricorn, 1959.

_____. *Notes on the State of Virginia.* New York: W. W. Norton, 1954.

Kimball, Marie. *Jefferson, the Road to Glory 1743 to 1776.* New York: Coward–McCann, 1943.

Koch, Adrienne. *Jefferson and Madison: The Great Collaboration.* London: Oxford University Press, 1980.

Levy, Leonard W. *Jefferson and Civil Liberties: The Darker Side.* Chicago: Elephant Paperbacks, Ivan R. Dee, 1989.

Lurton, Douglas E., ed. *The Jefferson Bible: The Life and Morals of Jesus of Nazareth.* New York: Henry Holt, 1995.

Malone, Dumas. *Jefferson and His Time.* Boston: Little, Brown, 1948.

Mapp, Alf J., Jr. *Thomas Jefferson: A Strange Case of Mistaken Identity.* Lanham, Maryland: Madison Books, 1989.

_____. *Thomas Jefferson: Passionate Pilgrim: The Presidency, the Founding of the University, and the Private Battle.* Lanham, Maryland: Madison Books, 1991.

McDonald, Forrest. *The Presidency of Thomas Jefferson.* Lawrence, Kansas: University Press of Kansas, 1976.

McLaughlin, Jack. *Jefferson and Monticello: The Biography of a Builder.* New York: Henry Holt, 1990.

Miller, John Chester. *The Wolf by the Ears: Thomas Jefferson and Slavery.* Charlottesville, Virginia: University Press of Virginia, 1991.

Morgan, Edmund S. *Virginians at Home: Family Life in the Eighteenth Century.* Williamsburg, Virginia: The Colonial Williamsburg Foundation, 1952.

Morse, John T., Jr. *American Statesmen: Thomas Jefferson.* Boston: Houghton Mifflin, 1911.

Olmstead, Frederick Law. *The Cotton Kingdom.* New York: Da Capo, 1996.

Onuf, Peter S. *Jeffersonian Legacies.* Charlottesville, Virginia: University Press of Virginia, 1993.

Padover, Saul K. *A Jefferson Profile: As Revealed in His Letters.* New York: John Day, 1956.

Peterson, Merrill D. *Adams and Jefferson: A Revolutionary Dialogue.* Oxford: Oxford University Press, 1978.

_____, ed. *The Portable Thomas Jefferson.* New York: Penguin Books, 1977.

Randall, Willard Sterne. *Thomas Jefferson: A Life.* New York: Henry Holt, 1993.

Wibberly, Leonard. *Man of Liberty: A Life of Thomas Jefferson.* New York: Farrar, Straus and Giroux, 1968.

Wolf, Stephanie Grauman. *As Various as Their Land: The Everyday Life of Eighteenth-Century Americans.* New York: HarperCollins, 1993.

Acknowledgments

Another Thomas with no middle name, Thomas Lumbard, friend for over forty years, brought me books and encouragement whenever the task I had set for myself seemed daunting. Without him, this book might still be a half-finished first draft, resting moribund in a rarely opened file drawer.

Dorothy Briley of Clarion Books gave new vitality to the project when she accepted it for publication. For help in picture research I thank the staff at Colonial Williamsburg, the Virginia Historical Society in Richmond, the Special Collections Department at the University of Virginia Library, and research assistant Rebecca Bowman and director Dan Jordan at Monticello. Thanks are also due the Library of Congress, especially director of Prints and Photographs Mary Ison.

For her keen eye and astute judgment in picture selection, as well as her support in many other ways, I offer loving gratitude to my wife, Sylvia.

John B. Severance

Index

Page numbers in *italics* refer to photos or captions.